THE TOURISTS GAZE,
THE CRETANS GLANCE

Heritage, Tourism, and Community

Helaine Silverman, *University of Illinois, Urbana-Champaign*

SERIES EDITOR

The innovative volumes in the Heritage, Tourism, and Community series confront these interconnected issues from multidisciplinary and interdisciplinary perspectives, addressing heritage and tourism and their relationships to local community, economic development, regional ecology, heritage conservation and preservation, and related indigenous, regional, and national political and cultural issues. Of particular interest are policy parameters and implications for affected communities; issues of representation; different meanings and understandings of heritage held by different stakeholders that revolve around sites and performances; gender issues, from tourism's differential impact on communities to how men and women travel; and the role of various brokers such as tour guides and travel agents. The volumes in this series are all single-author case studies that convey the key elements of a specific case of heritage tourism development and highlight the value of the case to those in the heritage field. They are driven by both theory and practical principles drawn from the cases that demonstrate the book's relevance to critical issues in the field, and they make comparisons to other relevant case studies.

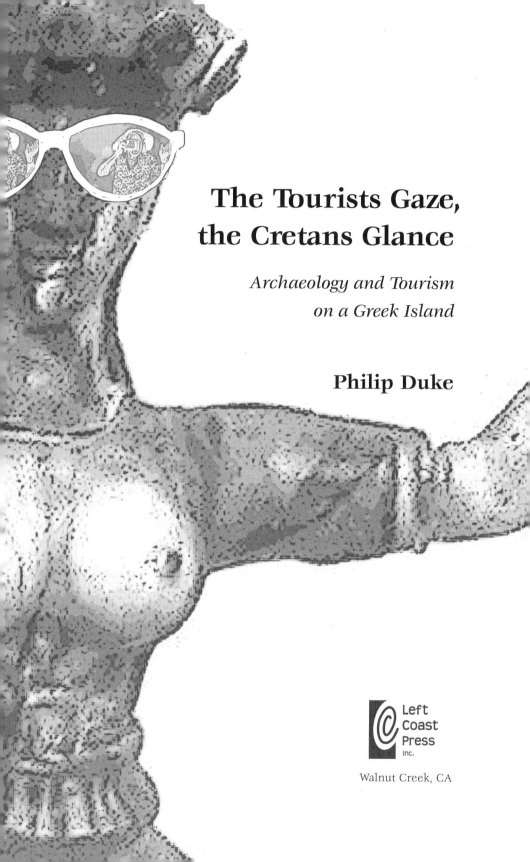

The Tourists Gaze, the Cretans Glance

Archaeology and Tourism on a Greek Island

Philip Duke

Left Coast Press inc.

Walnut Creek, CA

Left Coast Press, Inc.
1630 North Main Street, #400
Walnut Creek, California 94596
http://www.lcoastpress.com

Library of Congress Cataloging-in-Publication Data

Duke, P. G.
The tourists gaze, the Cretans glance : archaeology and tourism on a Greek island / Philip Duke.
p. cm. -- (Heritage, tourism and community)
Includes bibliographical references and index.
ISBN 978-1-59874-142-1 (hardback : alk. paper) -- ISBN 978-1-59874-143-8 (pbk. : alk. paper)
1. Crete (Greece)--Antiquities. 2. Minoans. 3. Tourism--Greece--Crete.
I. Title. II. Title: Archaeology and tourism on a Greek island.
DF221.C8D88 2007
939'.18--dc22
2007025217

07 08 09 5 4 3 2 1

Printed in the United States of America

The paper used in this publication meets the minimum requirements of American National Standard for Information Sciences—Permanence of Paper for Printed Library Materials, ANSI/NISO Z39.48—1992.

Text and cover design by Lisa Devenish.

Left Coast Press Inc. is committed to preserving ancient forests and natural resources. We elected to print *The Tourists Gaze, The Cretans Glance* on 30% post consumer recycled paper, processed chlorine free. As a result, for this printing, we have saved:

2 Trees (40' tall and 6-8" diameter)
890 Gallons of Wastewater
358 Kilowatt Hours of Electricity
98 Pounds of Solid Waste
193 Pounds of Greenhouse Gases

Left Coast Press Inc. made this paper choice because our printer, Thomson-Shore, Inc., is a member of Green Press Initiative, a nonprofit program dedicated to supporting authors, publishers, and suppliers in their efforts to reduce their use of fiber obtained from endangered forests.

For more information, visit www.greenpressinitiative.org

For DGD
For putting up with TSB

CONTENTS

PREFACE

by Helaine Silverman, Series Editor

As I was conducting a series of archaeological projects on the south coast of Peru in the 1980s and '90s I was frequently visited by tourists, documentary filmmakers, municipal authorities, and local townsfolk, each of whom expressed curiosity about, opinions concerning, and stakes in the ancient past of the region. This repeated experience eventually led me to turn away from archaeological excavation to archaeological ethnography, so to speak—to a study of the uses of the past in the present as conceived and asserted by a range of individuals and groups. This broad topic encompasses issues that have assumed paramount importance among a growing group of scholars: archaeologists and anthropologists, as well as cultural theorists in fields as diverse as history, architectural history, landscape architecture, geography, art history, classics, and urban planning, to name only the most obvious. All of us share an interest in the intersections of identity formation, community building, cultural heritage, nationalism, economic development, tourism, the built environment, localism and globalization, and, of course, ancient societies.

Heritage, Tourism, and Community is an innovative new book series that addresses the interconnected issues of heritage tourism and community development from multidisciplinary and interdisciplinary perspectives. The premise of the series is that archaeological and historic sites, specific buildings, museums of various types, performances, and natural environments are all venues for the construction and display of heritage by the tourism industry and by communities (up to the level of the imagined community of the nation), sometimes in consort with or opposition to each other. Of particular interest are policy parameters and policy implications for the affected communities.

Also important to consider are recursive issues of representation: how "others" are represented to tourists and how tourists are perceived by the willing or reluctant host community; the different meanings and understandings of heritage held by different stakeholders that revolve around sites and performances; class and gender issues; and the role of various brokers such as tour guides and travel agencies.

Many communities around the world, including in the United States, are building and claiming their heritage on the basis of tourist attractions or sites and performances that they wish to develop as tourist destinations. Tourism today is recognized as the world's greatest global industry in terms of revenue generated and human movement. In First World countries and the developing world, tourism is dramatically affecting the lives and livelihoods of surrounding populations and the economic and political strategies of the nation-states in which they are embedded. Even remote villages seek to market themselves as tourist attractions on the basis of noteworthy sites or traditional cultural performances, regions within a country compete with each other for tourists, and entire countries spend lavishly on slick ads in upscale magazines in an attempt to capture a major share of tourism's dividends.

The theoretically complex and pragmatically complicated intersections of heritage, tourism, and community offer an exciting intellectual space for dialogue, with application to real world situations. It is in this context that we are pleased to offer Philip Duke's *The Tourists Gaze, the Cretans Glance: Archaeology and Tourism on a Greek Island* as the first volume in the series.

Duke sensitively, creatively, and comprehensively interrogates tourism on Crete, drawing on his many years of archaeological and anthropological fieldwork. His study is all the more fascinating because Michael Herzfeld's important study of historical conservation and tourism on Crete (*A Place in History*:1991), from the perspective of the town of Rethymno, did not consider the Minoan past in terms of Cretan "social and monumental time." Thus, Duke provides us with the other, vitally important dimension for understanding identity construction, tourism, and ambiguous modernity on the island.

Duke is fundamentally interested in the Minoan past as a meta-narrative for Western social inequality, and in the packaging and perception/reception of the Minoan past and the degree and nature of the tourist's agency in engaging it. Monumental Knossos, as a metaphor for a past and present, is necessarily the preeminent site for interrogation as much of colonialist archaeological practice as modern tourist behavior and Greek identity ideologies at the local and national level. Of particular value for the nonspecialist is Duke's synthetic treatment of Minoan archaeology, a gem in itself. But it is precisely the fascinating prehistory of Crete that makes its tourism so interesting, for Duke has found that most tourists arrive on the island for sun and beaches rather than ancient walls and dusty museums. Indeed, although the tourist has sought out the exotic by going to Crete in the first place, nevertheless—much in the *Shirley Valentine* vein—the exotic must be packaged in strictly controlled environments, be it the ruins or the island's inhabitants. Duke critically examines the ambiguities and difficulties of the mediated tourist-host borderzone in this regard by a close reading of the verbal and visual media of tourism authority.

Through a work of applied archaeological ethnography Duke marvelously negotiates his way between the subjective and objective. His inclusion of selected diary notes, tables analyzing tourist facilities, and guidebooks at more than a dozen sites is highly original and establishes new worthwhile methodologies for this kind of study. His comparative discussion of market-oriented cultural heritage exploitation and socially focused and community owned heritage use raises issues that should be considered by all parties involved with archaeological sites and tourism. This group includes archaeologists who cannot and must not ignore the political and social ramifications of their work.

The Tourists Gaze, the Cretans Glance: Archaeology and Tourism on a Greek Island will surely stimulate discussion and promote further scholarly attention to the role of heritage exploitation in today's globalized world of tourism and commodification.

INTRODUCTION

*Well, yes, I have heard of Knossos. And there is a
big site on the south coast, right? No, I don't know
of this Kato Zakro.* (Cretan)

*They are our crown jewels, the reason why we are
famous, yes?* (Cretan)

*I didn't get to any of the sites, the beaches and bars
were too much fun.* (Tourist)

The last twenty-five years have seen archaeology take its first steps toward adulthood. As the processualist quest to make the discipline an
objective science has become more and more problematical, there has
been an increasing recognition that the past is a partially subjective
construction of the present. Archaeologists engage in a dialogue with
the past and the present, and ultimately with the *presence* of the past
expressed in the objects we excavate and put on display. As Shanks and
Tilley (1987:75) have noted, "[t]he notion of presence is at the heart of
the 'romance' of archaeology. . . . This presence constitutes the object's
authority, its authenticity." Ontologically separated at birth, the present
was once considered by archaeologists useful only for helping interpret
its sibling, the past, by providing models from the likes of ethnography,
economics, and geography. Now the relation is seen as altogether more
complex. For now we realize the siblings are Siamese twins and were
never separated at birth at all, and so we appeal to the present not
so much in these traditional ways, but rather to understand in hindsight why we constructed the archaeological past the way we did in
the first place and to understand how constructions of the past are so

thoroughly contextualized in the present. We recognize the importance of contemporary politics, class, gender, indigeneity, cultural identity, heritage, and globalism, and recognize that the archaeological past our predecessors labored so much to uncover was not so much a foreign country (a là Lowenthal [1985]) as a living colony whose inhabitants are forced to live by our rules. Now we embrace new disciplines for insight and guidance. We are comfortable with structuralism and post-structuralism, modernism and post-modernism, phenomenology, and all sorts of French philosophers who would have had our undergraduate supervisors of the 1970s reaching for the nearest gun.

This book is about a past but it is firmly situated in the present. It provides a case study of the past/present nexus and its impact on a group of people, tourists, who briefly tour a specific colony of the past, the Minoan Bronze Age. My claim is that public archaeology on Crete, manifested in sites and museums and the vast array of tourist information media, produces a virtually monolithic message about a particular past and thereby about a particular present; namely, that social inequality is the essential metanarrative of the Minoan past and thus abets in the legitimization and naturalization of this same social inequality as the primary organizational structure of the modern West. In this case study I contend that the particular form of social inequality revealed so powerfully to tourists is the inequality of socioeconomic class. This is of particular significance because while other voices are currently—and rightly—being given an audience in contemporary archaeological discourse (feminist and indigenous voices, especially) a "class" voice has been and continues to be undervalued in archaeology.

Tourism is a useful entry point into an evaluation of the present and its reconstitution in the past because of the latter's increasing prominence in the contemporary marketing of foreign countries as destinations for Western tourists. The tourist industry continues to co-opt the archaeological past for its own purposes, and has thus entered into the contestation of different constituencies over how the past is treated, interpreted, and stewarded. Although tourism is a form of culture contact with the Other (Howell 1994:151), it received little anthropological attention until relatively recently; Dennison Nash's work in the 1980s, when it was "still in its infancy" (Nash 1981:461), was amongst the first to advocate an explicitly anthropological study of tourism. One reason for this was perhaps that the study was simply seen as somewhat frivolous and not sufficiently intrepid for the hardy anthropological researcher (Nash 1981:461). Subsequent anthropological studies tended to emphasize tourism's impact on host communities, rather than the impact on the cultures and societies to which tourists return, perhaps unsurprisingly given the discipline's traditional focus on the Other. The call of Nash and Smith (1991:18) "to investigate further the 'nature' of the changes . . . that the tourists exhibit and relate them to their life at home" has only partly been answered (Nash 1996:163). This present study, looking at the impact that archaeological sites, museums, and the constructed past have on tourists in how they subsequently view their own culture, fits well into the type of study that Nash and Smith have called for. The issues I raise in this book are hardly unique to Crete. Tourism and its co-optation of heritage are global phenomena, and one small island can serve as an example of these phenomena. Moreover, many of the forces that determine tourist and heritage strategies originate outside of Greece and are rooted in the contemporary transnational economic system. Looking at Crete specifically, therefore, allows us an access to local realities without losing "sight of the global strategy which is imposed at local level" (to use Lanfant's phrase [1995:4]). My conclusions will, I trust, have resonance in any region where the past is used to entice tourists.

Let me pursue a little further, if only for didactic purposes, the colony as a metaphor for the past. The literature is replete with studies of how third world countries, many of them former European colonies, have discovered the economic benefits of tourism. A common strategy in entertaining tourists is to provide some deliberately staged dance or performance as a means of getting to know the host culture. However, this exposure must always be conducted in a strictly controlled environment so that a balance is always maintained between the exotic and the familiar. For example, Bruner (2005:87) has shown how tourists visiting the Maasai "receive drinks, food, a good show, an occasion to socialize, a chance to express their privileged status, an opportunity to experience vicariously the adventure of colonial Kenya, and a confirmation of their prior image of Africa." It is not too much of a stretch to suggest that the tourist on Crete (Greece is by no means a third world country, but the strategy remains the same) is, in similar fashion, offered archaeological sites and museums as a performance, an entertaining pageant full of mystery, wonder, and myth, glossed to be sure with the apparent certitude of science, but nevertheless ultimately a performance to be enjoyed. At the same time, tourists are very often isolated in modern hotels and only temporarily thrust into contact with the Other via a visit to an archaeological site or museum. Here, in a place very akin to what Bruner (2005:17) has appositely called a touristic borderzone, they are temporarily confronted with something that is not so exotic as to make them feel uncomfortable, and not so different as to be unknowable. Just as colonizing powers tried to refit their subjects into their own image, so we too with the past. This balancing act, as it were, between the exotic and the familiar is something I will return to throughout this book.

As the study progressed, it gradually changed from my original conception, a broadly etic *Foucaultian* analysis of archaeological knowledge and power, to a more experiential and personal engagement with a particular past. Therefore, at this point I must expose my own biases (if that is the right word), which are inescapably built into this study. There are advantages to this. Using "[a]n openly autobiographical style . . . at least . . . enables the reader to review his or her position to make the adjustments necessary for dialogue" (MacCannell 1992:10), and paradoxically, as MacCannell (1992:9) further notes, it "leads in the direction of scholarly objectivity, detachment, and neutrality." Rosemary Joyce (2002) has perceptively described archaeological writing as personal praxis. I could add personal catharsis to the list of advantages this style provides. Hodder (1999:194; 2003), in his work at Catal Huyuk, has focused on involving the local community in the creation of the archaeological past, and he acknowledges also that this reflexivity can lead to a healthy recognition of the archaeologist's own hidden assumptions about the past (Hodder 1999:194). The danger of publicly airing this self-awareness is a narcissistic monologue that illuminates little more than the writer's personal background, psychological profile, and so forth. Some of the recent works of Shanks (2004) and Tilley (2004) step close to this solipsistic precipice, with Shanks showing an inordinate amount of interest in three rooms that *speak* to him, and Tilley phenomenologically projecting his own reading of an ancient landscape west of Salisbury, England, in order to understand round barrows and dykes as landscape metaphors. However, reflexivity can also lead to remarkable insights on how the past is constructed and its profound influence on how the present is then understood. Engendered and indigenous archaeologies have moved the discipline to a greater social and political responsibility precisely because of their explicitly personal stance in understanding how the past has been constructed and contested.

I began my interest in archaeology with an infatuation with Greece. The country's past was my first intellectual love, and I use the noun deliberately. I adored Leonard Cottrell, especially *The Lion Gate* (1967, first published in 1963), and even Dilys Powell's *The Villa Ariadne* (2001, first published in 1973) and *An Affair of the Heart* (1973, first published in 1957), despite their suspiciously having too much of the *Little England* attitude to them, are still enjoyable. For a wide-eyed teenager in a dreary working-class section of Liverpool, escape would be running to the local library, and while the cold winter (and sometimes summer, as I remember) storms dashed against the windows I would look through glossy books on the magical fairy tale place called Greece. I poured over the elitist texts of Jacquetta Hawkes (she was a staple of the *Ancient History* section) and stared in awe at pictures of the Parthenon, the Lion's Gate, and Knossos. At the time, of course, I was not aware that the texts or the choice of photographs were elitist; that revelation would come much later.

While I was in high school, the study of ancient Greek and Latin took me further into this wonderful world, but I gave it all up at Cambridge to study *real* archaeology, that is, scientific archaeology, under the likes of Eric Higgs and David Clarke. I learned how the truth of the past could be established, and how famous sites could be placed in their proper long-term, systemic perspective. There were to be no great men, no great sites in this view of the past; all were simply manifestations of supra-human processes and dictates. Even though the two anthropologists were never mentioned in lectures (they were Americans, you know), Alfred Kroeber's superorganic and Leslie White's culturology ruled. My graduate work took me farther from Greece, to the University of Calgary and the mountains and plains of western North America, and finally to the dry deserts of the Four Corners, where I have lived, taught, and researched the past for the last twenty-seven years. There, from American Indian tribal elders, I learned of the overwhelming power of the past in shaping the present and in helping form how the future will be written, and my intellectual paradigms began to change.

My journey took me far away from my roots, and I can no longer consider myself working class. Yet I would be dishonest were I to assert that I am no longer influenced by my former membership of that class, for my own past still lurks in the undergrowth. It still influences the way in which I look at how the archaeological past is constructed and how the craft of archaeology is conducted (see also Minh-ha [1989:12–13] and Ryan and Sackrey [1996] for analogous discussions). The narrative I offer in this book is personal and understandable only within the context of a trialogue (cf. Bakhtin 1981, 1984) made up of myself, the reader, and all the others who past and present have already assigned meaning to the words and concepts I employ. Of these three parties, the only one I can possibly have any real understanding of or control over is myself. Nevertheless, I assume that even though I speak only for myself, my take on the past might well resonate with others'. It is not vanity that persuades me to think this. My reading of what sites and museums might evoke in casual visitors is not pulled out of thin air. It is pulled from a cultural frame of reference that is shared by others, if only partially.

This study became a very personal journey that involved not just me but also all the colleagues, friends, acquaintances, and strangers who contributed in all sorts of ways, large and small, to my narrative. It also involved responses—some of them admittedly subjective on my part—to the academic treatises, guide books, and tourist brochures (to name just a few) that I read. So, it should be seen partly as a self-ethnography, for I am my own informant. It is a journey that takes the reader down all sorts of avenues, from professional studies, journals, and books to personal observations and conclusions that to me at least nevertheless seem right. Clifford and Marcus's (1986) edited volume *Writing Culture: The Poetics and Politics of Ethnography* was one of the first works to expose for anthropologists the problematical relationship that exists between the subject matter, the reader, and the writer of ethnographic accounts, and we can substitute archaeological for ethnographic quite easily in this sentence. Trinh T. Minh-ha's (1989) *Woman, Native, Other* should convince the most hardened skeptic of self-ethnography's utility as a mode of analysis. Michael Herzfeld's *A Place in History* (1991) provided a model for discourse that seemed to fit what I was trying to do. In this monumental study Herzfeld dissected how the community in the old quarter of Rethymno in western Crete has come to terms with living in a heritage goldfish bowl while also coping with a tourist economy and an often intransigent heritage bureaucracy based in Athens. I was also attracted to the type of discourse exemplified in the *anthropological history* of the mutiny on the HMS Bounty written by Greg Dening (1992), *Mr Bligh's Bad Language: Passion, Power and Theatre on the Bounty*. In all of these studies the personal is never far from the surface.

The fieldwork for this project began in March and April of 2002, while on a sabbatical leave funded by Fort Lewis College and the State of Colorado Excellence Grant fund. As I have returned to the island each year since, I have added to my store of observations and these have reinforced my original suspicions. The format of this book is part archaeological and part ethnographic discourse. For archaeological matters I have used a variety of published sources, as well as professional and personal observations made by myself and others. During my stay on Crete I chose to rent a private apartment in Rethymno rather than one of the foreign school dormitories, mostly because I wanted to savor the island without the inevitable filter of an academic enclave. I made several friends during my stay. Some were academics, others were shop owners and university students working part-time, with little if any formal knowledge of the island's archaeological past. During my stay on the island informal conversations with these and other people I happened to end up chatting with over coffee or waiting in line for a bus, for example, gave me additional insights into how the Cretan past is understood. I never interviewed any of them as ethnographic informants, yet they provided interesting insights that sometimes took me down new avenues.

Chapter 1 introduces the reader to a detailed exposure of the line of argument I follow in this book. Chapter 2 discusses the present state of Bronze Age archaeology on Crete in order to provide a baseline for helping determine what is and what is not offered to tourists. Chapter 3 investigates tourism and how tourists interact with the cultures both past and present into which they have been temporarily thrown. Chapter 4 examines the different sources of information available to the tourist about Bronze Age archaeological sites on Crete and the different media by which the past is presented. Chapter 5 presents explanations for the voices and silences that characterize the constructed past. These explanations are situated within an evaluation of both the current status and the historical development of Minoan archaeology as an academic discipline, as well as nonacademic but equally powerful forces, such as the economic needs of the country and the historical phenomena of colonialism/imperialism and nationalism. In this chapter the different hegemonies that create the stratigraphic palimpsest of meaning about the Minoan past are excavated. Chapter 6 stands back and places this study into a more global context.

A note on the book's title is in order. The term *Cretan Glance* was coined by Nikos Kazantsakis, Crete's most famous literary son. He used it to describe the Cretans' ability to deal with the present and to look to the future—to death even—with acceptance, fortitude, a near insouciance. But it struck me also as a particularly apt way of describing how so many Cretans I talked to saw their past; it is here, it happened, it is a source of pride, but they must look beyond it to face the real challenges of their lives. *Tourist Gaze* is the title of a stimulating book by John Urry (1990). It struck me as an apposite way of describing how most tourists look at the cultures into which they have been briefly catapulted: an uncomprehending—even open-mouthed—appraisal of the Other (but see also Bruner's [2005:95] *questioning gaze*).

Acknowledgments

I am eternally thankful for a department and a college that would allow one of its members to switch his teaching and research interests so drastically, from North America to Greece. During my sabbatical I was based at the University of Crete in Rethymno, and I am grateful to Olga Graziou, Iris Tzachili, and Anna Missiou for their warm hospitality and generous help. My traveling companion was my son, Tristan. I could not have asked for better company. A wizard at pulling gourmet meals from the thin air of our cramped kitchen, Tris also served as the project's photographer and provided other assistance in ways too numerous to mention. I am most deeply indebted to two colleagues. Yannis Hamilakis encouraged this project from its earliest glimmerings. He took the time to read and make comments on several versions of the manuscript and he helped to steer me through the often choppy waters of Minoan prehistory and its contemporary politics. Kathy Fine, my colleague at Fort Lewis College, read multiple drafts and offered many wise insights. Without the advice of these two colleagues, this work would be much poorer. I thank, too, Alice Kehoe, Chuck Riggs, Peter McCormick, Olga Krzyszkowska, Neil Brodie, Stella Galani, Manolis Karagiannakis, Sarah Cady Roberts, Mary Ann Erickson, and Bob Kimmick for their help and support. I am fortunate to have such friends and colleagues. I am especially grateful to Helaine Silverman, editor of this series, and Mitch Allen, publisher of LeftCoast Press, for their support of this project and their invaluable help in getting it to the light of day. I also gratefully acknowledge all those Minoan prehistorians, past and present, on whose scholarship I have relied so heavily. Finally, thanks to my old friend and colleague, Dean Saitta, who helps to keep the hope alive in me that archaeology can be socially and politically relevant. Unfortunately, none of these individuals can be held responsible for any shortcomings of this book. These must all be down to me.

CHAPTER ONE

Touring the Past

*To select only monuments suppresses at one stroke the
reality of the land and that of its people, it accounts for
nothing of the present, that is, nothing historical, and
as a consequence, the monuments themselves become
undecipherable, therefore senseless.*

Roland Barthes (1987:76), *Mythologies.*

Preamble

Knossos on a cool March day. Already, despite the earliness of the
season, the site is full of tourists, though nothing like the hordes that
will be there by June. In small groups of two or five, clutching guidebooks like the faithful grasp their rosaries, or in dutiful processions
of thirty or more as congregants in the mass, they move through the
site. Are they pilgrims at a holy site, waiting for their moment of revelation, or are they perhaps merely bored, wondering why they are
here but staying anyway? Do they stay out of respect, or awe, or mere
practicality because they don't know how to get back to the hotel by
themselves? Knossos directs them—and us—to a particular past, to a
particular present. But are they aware of this? What does this site, and
many others on the island, tell the visitor about their past and more
importantly about their present?

These questions plagued me as I made my own pilgrimages to the site
over the years. Was I simply being a cynical and jaded academic, who
secretly disparages the very people to whom he wants to make archaeology relevant, or was there in fact something to my musings? I became
animated by the need to investigate the nexus between archaeological sites and their visitors, and to understand exactly what information

about the past is on offer, and why. Tourism not only has the potential to make a significant contribution to a country's economy. When archaeological sites are actively used to attract tourists, tourism's tentacles can spread into the very cultural identity of that country to become "an arena where identities are created, reaffirmed and valorized, memories and visual signifiers produced and reproduced" (Hamilakis 2006:159). Thus, as Silverman (2002:883) has noted, "[a]rchaeological tourism provides the opportunity for selective re-creation and reconstruction of the past," and forces us to confront the construction of a past that is then selectively sold to the public. Who selects? Who controls? To what extent is the public treated merely as a passive consumer of knowledge?

A tourist who enters an archaeological site enters—literally and metaphorically—an intersection of contemporary and historical forces that have already begun to filter the information the tourist receives. The filter is composed of two sieves. The first is made by archaeologists whose selective interest in the past is contextualized within their own individual intellectual paradigms and ideologies. It goes virtually without saying that archaeologists are united in their concern for the protection of archaeological sites and the appropriate use of archaeological knowledge. Yet archaeology's nature as a privileged study has convinced many archaeologists, most certainly in the past but even today, that they alone are in the singular position of being able to interpret the remnants of the prehistoric past, so a real dialogue (versus a monologue) with the public about what the past means to and for that public is not a high priority. Certainly, as Russell (2006:25) has pointed out, many archaeologists and historians may actually fear the effects of the past's popularity with the public in that control over the past may be unnecessarily yielded or the past may be misunderstood. Only recently have archaeologists begun to recognize their roles in contemporary cultural production and to take responsibility for the consequences (albeit often unintended) of their actions and their pronouncements.

The second sieve is constructed by the choices made by site managers over what is presented to the public in terms of site access and presentation, and by the tourist industry, both state and private sector, which uses particular archaeological sites, museums, and artifacts—and thereby a particular past—to entice tourists to Crete. The tourist trade is one of Greece's most important sources of foreign currency, the country receiving each year more foreign tourists (over fourteen million in 2003) than its resident population, just under eleven million people. Greece, along with other countries such as Egypt, Italy, and Mexico, has one of the most well-developed industries in the world for attracting foreign tourists, and the Greek past is one of the more prominent tools in its armory. The website of the Greek National Tourist Organization (GNTO), for example, as well as the myriad marketing tools used by private-enterprise tourist packages, all prominently display ancient ruins or statues (clothed and naked), which occupy the pole position with sun and beaches for alluring tourists. It might be facile to see the tourist industry as a faceless and monolithic entity, coldly manipulating the past for its own profits, though sometimes one does wonder.

Crete offers specific advantages for the type of study in which I am engaged. First, it contains some of the most remarkable sites in Greece, including the site type for Minoan culture, Knossos, the most important archaeological site on Crete, one of the earliest draws in what we today call the heritage industry (McEnroe 2002:69), and also one of the most popular tourist attractions on the island. As many as 8,000 visitors a day, around one million visitors a year, descend on Knossos—figures exceeded in Greece only by visits to the Acropolis (Hamilakis 2002a:2; Papadopoulos 2005:120). Second, the island provides a well-defined archaeological laboratory from both a geographical and a cultural standpoint. Crete is a relatively small island—approximately 150 miles long and fifteen miles wide at its narrowest portion—and its Bronze Age cultures have been studied in detail for well over one hundred years, making it one of the most intensively studied archaeological areas in the world (Hamilakis 2002a:4). Although the island is geographically and culturally an ideal laboratory for archaeological study, it would be unwise to take this analogy too far, for doing so has led to the assumption that the island was characterized by far more cultural homogeneity than was actually the case. Yet somewhat surprisingly, despite the intensity of archaeological investigations on the island and the importance that Greece has in the construction of the ideological concept we term the *West*, the constitution and contestation of Crete's Minoan past has not perhaps received the attention it deserves (papers in Hamilakis [2002b] and Hamilakis and Momigliano [2006] are a noteworthy exception).[1]

This study is predicated on two contentions that need to be more fully aired before proceeding further. The first concerns why the past and present are indeed metaphorical Siamese twins that were never separated at birth. It is contended here that because we in the West conceive of time as proceeding inexorably from past, to present, to future (although the last never arrives), the only way we can make sense of the present is to compare it to what has gone before: "Our lives are a double helix of past and present," to use Dening's (1992:9) phrase. Thus, the relationship between past and present constitutes an unavoidable conundrum whereby each informs the other in an endless Mobius strip of meaning. But what do we mean when we say that the past is constructed? The past, as constituted by individual events, happened only once, and its material resistance does serve as a check on its portrayal (Wylie 1992). Therefore, constructing the past does not mean writing fiction, although critics would say that is exactly the turn some have made (for example, Binford [1989:*passim*]). Nor does it entail a slide into subjective hyper-relativism. Rather, our ability to select only certain aspects of the past as worthy of investigation means, for all practical purposes, that many different versions of the past, all of them having legitimacy, can be created. It is a shame that processual archaeology convinced many archaeologists to deny themselves that luxury. So, the question ultimately becomes not *what* past is recreated, but what *particular version* is created of the many pasts potentially available: what questions are asked and what answers are given (cf. Fabian 1983; Hodder 1986; Patterson 1986; Shanks and Tilley 1987; Layton 1989; Trigger 1989; Gathercole and Lowenthal 1994; Kehoe 1998; Silverman 2002). Yet traditional ways continue to dominate public access to the past. The past is recreated (that is, one version is turned into the only reality) by professionals—archaeologists, heritage managers, and the like. This single version is then presented to the public without the opportunity for dialogue or even questioning.

Arguing that the past can be manipulated, as it were, for particular ends requires first a definition of the archaeological record, the entity that is selectively offered to the public. Defining the record is a rather more complex issue than might appear at first blush (cf. Patrik 1985). The archaeological record is defined in introductory textbooks as "the physical remains produced by past human activities, which are sought, recovered, studied, and interpreted by archaeologists to reconstruct the past" (Ashmore and Sharer [2000:246], to use just one example.) Archaeologists have traditionally viewed this record as almost a natural entity that was deposited at some point in the past and now merely awaits the application of relevant methods and techniques to reconstruct the past human behavior it signifies. In traditional archaeology, not all elements of the archaeological record are deemed as worthy of investigation as others, and so for all intents and purposes unimportant elements are excluded from further analysis. Selection can be made by research archaeologists on the basis of particular research goals, for example. However, archaeologists increasingly have acknowledged, even in America, the bastion of scientific archaeology (Wylie 2002:246), that their own disciplinary values are not always paramount in selecting sites and deciding on their treatment and role. Government archaeology and heritage preservation concentrates on those elements of the record that fulfill their own particular mandates, and so the choices for site restoration are affected by state values and ideologies (Price 1994). The converse can apply: in reference to Greece, "lack of pro-active management can itself create a public perception of sites as being of low importance" (Wallace 2005:55). In the traditional view, the archaeological record exists as something outside of our own making, and the subsequent debate devolves to what is selected from that record as worthy of further study or preservation.

There is no need to slide down the slippery slope of hyper-relativism. Of course, sites and the artifacts in museums are real objects that were produced by past human behavior and are differentially preserved by the quirks of natural processes. However, that is emphatically not the archaeological record. The archaeological record is not something that exists outside of our universe of meaning. It is created by us with all our own academic, political, and personal interests in what we consider worth investigating (cf. Patrik 1985; Kotsakis 1999:97). Thus, there is a subtle—but crucial—difference between the archaeological record as something natural that exists outside our world and which we can only reconstruct and protect as its professional stewards—the traditional view—and the archaeological record as something created by us, whether archaeologists or not, as the product of social and cultural needs and ideologies, both past and present, explicit or not. Hamilakis (1999:60) has argued that archaeologists own up to their role "as intellectuals who deal with representation, rather than as stewards of the archaeological 'record'." In this view, the record is produced through "disciplinary practices and discourses on identity" and archaeologists must acknowledge their important role in cultural production. Therefore, academic and ideological decisions today and at the time of the sites' initial investigations determine what is examined, what is ignored, and thereby what constitutes the so-called record. Then, from this record, sites are selected for public access and at the same time certain sets of information are provided, others silenced. Therefore, it cannot in any reasonable way be argued that what gets finally to the public is objective or scientifically constituted.

Site stewardship deals with decisions on what sites and parts of sites are selected for preservation and public access. The traditional view of stewardship is that sites are part of our collective heritage (either national or Western) and, therefore, some of these sites are worthy of preservation for future generations. However, looking to the future subtly lets us off the hook regarding what we do with sites in the present. If sites are preserved for the future, then their potential role for contributing to our understanding of the present can be relegated in importance. One important ramification of this commitment to the future rather than to the present is that it allows public interpretation to be passive, uncontroversial, and anodyne. The past becomes uncontroversial, just the way the tourist industry wants it. Indeed, we can suggest that under this view, sites are corpses, and that the task of site stewardship is simply to develop the most effective embalming techniques. Consider Dening's (1992:4–5) take on *reenacting the past*, which really is what we try to do in the stewardship of archaeological sites: we "remove the responsibility of remedying the present by distracted, unreflective search for details of a past whose remedying will make no difference."

My second contention is that a visitor to a public site or museum is provided little opportunity to form his or her own opinion. Such loci are full of images and, as Graham Dann (1995:117) has argued, because "images (whether mental, verbal, or pictorial) are articulated sociolinguistically," they can "evoke a closed or focused discourse which draws on selective and sometimes exaggerated cultural markers in order to provide a mental grid for tourists to filter their perceptions and expectations." He has also compared tourists to children in that they give up their independent adult roles and are essentially led through the experience (Dann 1996). Dann was referring specifically to the authority figure of the hotel management, but we can appositely transfer his observations to the experience of the tourist on archaeological sites as well. The tourist is led passively through the site maze, along signposted walks on some sites, with simple diagrams and texts providing the minimum information necessary *to do* the site. He or she is exposed to well-rehearsed descriptions of the age of the sites, their construction history, and their most important *treasures*. The sites and museums do not offer anything to offend or indeed to make the tourist think of anything beyond their antiquity and their wondrousness. The past is simplified and sterilized. What could be an engaging dialog with a dynamic and ever-changing past becomes a synchronic moment, a fetish to be commodified, used, and then cast away. The site becomes dead, inert.

Arguing for the essential passivity of the public is risky, as it opens one to charges of assuming that the public is made up of dupes, incapable of putting their own *spin* on the past, incapable of negotiating with it, to use a popular term (and certainly the dearth of information on many archaeological sites on Crete provides the leeway for individual interpretations and conclusions to a degree not seen on more controlled sites).[2] Archaeologists such as Michael Shanks may believe that the visitor is not *duped* at all to think along certain lines in the way academics assume.[3] Mosei (2001) has argued that archaeological knowledge is constructed in a social context which itself is partially informed about the past by popular representations of that same past, implying that the individual as part of a larger group influences how the past is portrayed. Both of these studies credit the public with a great deal of individual and active thought.

Archaeological sites in this perspective are best not seen, then, simply as representations of past human behavior that merely await the appropriate methodologies for their essential truth to be spilled out. Nor are museums simply material repositories of the truths about the past. No, sites and museums are active collaborators in the present. They do have the power to speak in different voices, even if some of those voices have been temporarily muted.

However, perhaps part of the willingness to invest the tourist observer with free will is the result of some academics' needing to feel that they have not unnecessarily put the nonspecialist down—(amongst other criticisms leveled at Shanks and Tilley's early work [e.g., 1987] was their unwillingness to confront their own positions within a privileged institution of education [cf. Wylie 2002:276]). Moreover, given that the tourist is directed most often (either by pre-trip readings, in-country advice, or pre-arranged tours) to major sites such as Knossos, Phaistos, or Mallia, where control over the message is palpable, I would argue that the tourist has little input into the formation of knowledge about the past. I concede, of course, that archaeological sites do provide guidance to what they mean, minimal though the guidance may be, and not just in terms of the substantive facts about the sites (for example, its dates of occupation), but, more pertinently, about what is and what is not important about the sites and their past. However, as I have argued elsewhere (Duke 2006), a site like Knossos serves as a metaphor for a past and the present, and in so doing closes down debate about alternative pasts. The monumentality of the structures themselves combined with other media of information connote a scientific authority that is barely to be questioned. To adumbrate an example I will look at later on, how much could the typical tourist reasonably be expected to criticize the Knossos reconstruction and its consequent interpretation when the bust of Arthur Evans, its architect (and I use that noun deliberately), looms over every tourist entering the site and when he is praised in any and all guidebooks the visitor might have perused (Figure 1.1)?

Figure 1.1 *Bust of Arthur Evans*

The degree to which visitors are duped by physical monuments is explored in Mark Leone's (1987, 1988) study of William Paca's eighteenth century Maryland garden. Leone argued that the naturalized layout of Paca's garden enabled him and his visitors (members of his own class) to soothe the contradictions between his own slave-based wealth and his advocacy of human liberty. Leone's specific conclusions can be questioned (e.g., Hodder 1986:70), and certainly it is unproductive to think of his visitors totally as unthinking dupes. Nevertheless, any praxis the visitor has with the monument, be it an archaeological site on Crete or a Georgian garden in Maryland, is surely contextualized within a frame of reference established by the site itself. Barrett's (2000:762) critique of Wilkie and Bartoy's (2000) criticisms of Leone's so-called *Annapolis school* is telling:[4]

> class is made in the *real* physical conditions of history through the practices of agencies that have differential access to resources, act with different degrees of effect upon the world around them, and are stratified in relation to the ways they can work on identities and lives of others [emphasis added].

Therefore, to assert that no control is imposed on the site visitor at all would be naïve, to say the least; "the past is a rule-governed, therefore finite cultural resource. As with other kinds of cultural rules, *anything is possible, but only some things are permissible*" (Appadurai 1901:210, emphasis added). Visitors are not totally free agents, and the intellectual authority that subtly permeates archaeological sites is not an abstraction that can simply be thought away. So, archaeological sites and museums can justifiably be viewed as powerful tools that structure how visitors think about the past and thereby the present, without having to relegate those visitors to unthinking dupes capable of no negotiation with the past at all.

In making my case in the remainder of this book, I lay out what knowledge has been produced about the Cretan Bronze Age and why only certain questions about the past have been addressed, and then compare that knowledge to what is presented to the public at sites and museums. This will then allow me to identify the voices and the silences about the Minoan past. What is communicated to the public when Knossos, for instance, is referred to as a palace? That class structure is the basis of Europe's first civilization? What is communicated when knowledge of Bronze Age gender roles or social tensions is overlooked in favor of a picture of happy Minoans living under the beneficent rule of the palaces? That these are unimportant topics? And if these issues are not worth mentioning in a society that is projected in much of the tourist literature—accurately or not—as the basis of subsequent Western civilization, could it not be unconsciously inferred, therefore, that they are unimportant today in our own culture? And so just as the processual use of systems analysis could unconsciously legitimate the social status quo and treat social disruption as pathological (Shanks and Tilley 1987:53), class inequality is legitimated as the natural form of social organization in the West.

If the specific disparities between what is known by professional archaeologists and what is then presented to the public can be identified, a more challenging task is to unpack the reasons behind them. This involves delving into the cognitivist and noncognitivist factors that determined the development of Minoan archaeology, the former emphasizing "the substance of research," the latter focusing on political, ideological, and other similar forces (cf. Morris 1994:9). The investigation will take us all the way back to the late nineteenth and early twentieth centuries, when Bronze Age Crete was proclaimed to be "the cradle of European civilization" (Evans 1921:24), and the island was virtually divided into scholarly fiefdoms, each run by individual foreign schools,

mainly the British, French, Italian, and American (McEnroe 2002:61).
I do not conduct my investigation, however, as Kristiansen (1992:10)
writes, "with the object of exercising ideological criticism, since it is
relatively easy with hindsight to identify false conclusions and hidden
ideological messages." Kristiansen, as I read him, is suggesting that it is
relatively easy to come up with the end-result. The end result is important, of course, but the end-result is merely the result of deeper historical and contemporary forces, and it is these that I hope to uncover as I
pick apart the threads that make up the fabric of Minoan archaeology.
I must examine the status of contemporary Minoan archaeology and
also the nonacademic context within which is situated the construction and public presentation of the Minoan past, a context that includes
colonialism/imperialism, the aesthetic of modernity, nationalism, and
the economic dictates of modern Greece. I also cannot ignore the Cretans themselves, the people who work in hotels and bars or drive taxis
and tour buses, and so on—the people of the island without whom the
service industry would quickly collapse. For these people, despite the
pervasive insulation that most tourists have from the local population,
often can informally provide information on what to do on Crete, which
archaeological sites to visit, and what the tourist will see there. Therefore, it is important to try to gauge what they themselves think of the
Minoan past and how the constructed Minoan past has been integrated
into their own perceptions of identity, both national and local, if only as
a counterpoint to what is actually on offer to the foreign tourists temporarily dwelling on the touristic borderzone of past and present.

NOTES

1. Ethnographic studies by Herzfeld (1991) in Rethymno and Malaby (2003) in
    Chania, although concerned with contestation, have restricted themselves
    to what one might call the historical present.

2. This debate is not unique to public archaeology; tourism studies reveal the
    same issues. So, for example, Cohen (1988) has assigned the tourist virtu-
    ally total free will, while Boorstin (1964) portrayed the tourist simply as
    a dupe of the establishment. Urry's original phrase *the tourist gaze*, which
    was meant to describe the tourist's near acquiescence to what he or she is
    offered, has become under Bruner (2005: 95) the *questioning gaze* in recogni-
    tion of the "tourists' doubt about the credibility, authenticity, and accuracy
    of what is presented to them."

3. Mike Shanks made this criticism in a symposium that I had jointly organized with Yannis Hamilakis at the World Archaeological Congress, Washington, D.C. (2003). He objected to my characterization of tourists as incapable of making their own decisions about site interpretation. While I respected his comment, I thought it a bit rich coming from someone who co-wrote *Reconstructing Archaeology*.

4. Mark Leone has relied on critical theory as a tool to reveal the political implications of all archaeological work. He and his colleagues initially explored the implications of this approach through long-term excavations and analysis of historical Annapolis on the eastern seaboard of the United States.

CHAPTER TWO

The Minoan Past

*Diligently working upon the refuse-heaps of some
township for a number of years [archaeologists] erect on
the basis of a few sherds or a piece of dramatic drainage,
a sickly and enfeebled portrait of a way of life. How true
it is, we cannot say.*

Lawrence Durrell (1996:59; original 1945), *Prospero's Cell*.

This chapter summarizes the archaeology of the Minoan period, in order better to situate the discussions that follow in Chapters 4 and 5. It
is not intended as a comprehensive review; whole books are devoted to
this. Rather, I wish to isolate some of the salient features of the Cretan
Bronze Age and to highlight some of the debates and uncertainties that
surround an archaeological culture that after over a century of study
still is seemingly characterized by as much darkness as light. Whenever
scholars describe the contemporary study of an area as reflective of
"interesting times," as Day and Relaki (2002:217) have done for Crete,
then you know that most things are still up for grabs. There is a press-
ing need to deinsularize the island, not so much in terms of explicating
more fully the myriad cultural relationships between Minoan culture
and the rest of the Aegean—important though this is—but rather in
terms of bringing Minoan studies more into mainstream archaeology
(Hamilakis 2002b:17) without losing the essential uniqueness that Minoan studies have acquired over the last century.[1] I begin this chapter
with a description of the natural environment of the island as the context in which Bronze Age culture developed.

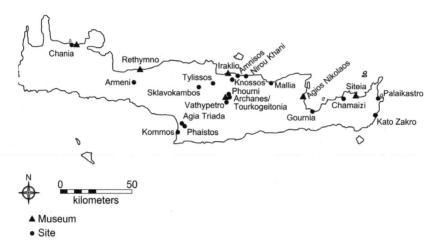

Figure 2.1 *Sites and Museums Visited*

The Natural Environment

Crete is the southernmost of the Greek islands, lying some 3000 miles from the Libyan coast (Figure 2.1). The largest of the Greek islands, it is approximately 156 miles in length (west to east). The island has a maximum width of about 36 miles and narrows down to less than 10 miles at the isthmus of Ierapetra, in the east end of the island. The total land area comprises about 3,240 square miles. Its coastline is 656 miles long but affords only a few natural harbors.

The climate is characterized as Mediterranean: hot, dry summers and mild, wet winters, the result of the conjunction of four weather systems. During the summer the Azores high and the Indo-Persian low together create northerly *meltemis*. During the winter the North Atlantic low and the high-pressure system over North Africa create westerlies over the island (Rackham and Moody 1996:33–34). Mean temperatures at Chania, as an example, range from 53.4⁰ F in January to 80.4⁰ F in July (Rackham and Moody 1996:36). Temperatures fall approximately 11⁰ F for every 3,000 feet of ascent. Winters are wet, with rain in the lower elevations and snow falling in the mountains and sometimes staying on the higher peaks well into the summer months. The west of the island tends to be wetter than areas to the east. Just about all precipitation falls between October and March (Davaras 1976:53). Only ten small rivers flow perennially (Rackham and Moody 1996:41), and there is a small lake, Lake Kournas (160 acres), west of Rethymno.

Crete is a land of mountains and plains. The mountains, the south-ernmost extension of the Dinaric Alps, are comprised mainly of lime-stone and form three principal masses: the White Mountains at the western end of the island; Mount Psiloriti (Mount Ida) in the middle; and the Lasithi Mountains to the east. The highest elevations are found in the first two ranges, with Mount Psiloriti, the very highest, having an altitude of 9,056 feet above sea level. Fifty-seven peaks have elevations over 3,300 feet. The mountains are pocked with caves, some very small but others large enough to have served as the location of habitation sites or shrines (Rackham and Moody 1996:25). Plains remain important lo-cations for arable production, as they did in prehistoric times. The larg-est is the Plain of Mesara, found on the southern part of the island. Crete also boasts high upland plains, the most significant being Omolos and Lasithi. Much of the island is covered by a type of limestone known to the islanders as *kouskouras*. Crete does not have many ore resources, but these include copper, iron, lead, manganese, and lignite.

The island lies on a tectonic zone of transition (Gifford 1992:17; Rackham and Moody 1996:13), and this, together with global changes in sea levels over the last five thousand years (Gifford 1992:23), has resulted in the Minoan coastline in the central and eastern sections of the island lying several meters lower than today's (Gifford 1992:23). Tectonic activity and eustatic sea level changes have resulted in dif-ferent effects on archaeological sites depending on their locations. Parts of sites at Matala and Olous, for example, lie beneath sea level. The harbor of Greek Phalasarna by contrast is well above present sea level (Rackham and Moody 1996:200).

Climatic complexity, together with severe altitudinal variation over short distances, has resulted in great biotic diversity. Moody (1997:62) succinctly describes the island as "a mini-continent with environments ranging from sub-tropical to temperate, to arctic—all within 30 km of each other." There are over 139 plant species native to Crete. The wild vegetation of contemporary Crete is dominated by *phrygana*, low-growing shrubs with hard leaves and sometimes spiny growth. Other important plants include the iris, narcissus, lily, saffron, poppy, and a variety of herbs useful in both cooking and medicine. Much of the island is de-voted to olive and wine production, and cultivation over the millennia, combined with deforestation for ships' timbers and house construction (Crete was famous in antiquity for its cypress trees [Cadogan 1992a:31]) and overgrazing by sheep and goats, has radically changed the natural environment of the island. The greatest loss is that of the extensive for-ests of cypress, plane, fir, juniper, maple, and oak that once blanketed the island. Wooded areas are now confined mostly to the area near Chania. Smaller pockets of oak, carob, and conifer are found throughout the island. No pollen cores exist from Crete during the Late Bronze Age (Moody 1997:71). However, elsewhere in Europe there is evidence for glacial advances, so Crete may have experienced a colder climate at that time (ibid). Mainland Greek pollen cores show an increase in arboreal species (ibid). Indigenous fauna include the *agrimi*, a feral wild goat that is now confined to the mountains and not often seen, and which was probably introduced during the Minoan period (Rackham and Moody 1996:47). In the prehistoric period wild animals included wolves, foxes, bears, boar, wild cattle, deer, and perhaps even lions, rabbits, hares, weasels, badgers and martens, pigeon, pheasant, partridge, hoopoe, and quail.

Minoan Culture History

The period on which this book concentrates (approximately 2000 to 1000 B.C.) is a division of the Bronze Age, which refers to a period from approximately 3000 to 1000 B.C. (depending on the specific location), when European societies had mastered and relied heavily on bronze metallurgy. The study of Aegean Bronze Age archaeology began with excavations at Troy in northwest Turkey in 1870 and later at Mycenae on the Greek mainland in 1876, by the self-taught archaeologist Heinrich Schliemann. His excavations, their crudity notwithstanding, demonstrated (1) that the region contained significant prehistoric cultures, that is, with high-quality material culture and complex architecture; and (2) that there was some historical basis to the Homeric epics (proving their accuracy had been his goal in excavating these sites to begin with).

No excavations were conducted on Crete until the latter part of the nineteenth century (Platon 1962:15). Minoan archaeology (named after the legendary King Minos) began as a formal academic study in the late nineteenth century with the excavation and subsequent reconstruction of Knossos (Figure 2.2) by Arthur Evans, who had been lured to the site by the numerous seals that had been unearthed there. He procured the rights to excavate by the simple expedient of buying the land the site was on, despite competition from other archaeologists (Hamilakis 2002a:2). In 1883 Schliemann had tried to buy Knossos preparatory to his anticipated excavation, but even he felt the price was too high (*Athena Review* 2003a); his well-known wealth apparently led to some price-gouging by the site's owners (Lapatin 2002:44). Moreover, his timing was not right, as Hazzidakis and other powerful parties on the island did not want any excavations while the island was still controlled by the Ottomans (Papadopoulos 2005:96). Evans felt that he had unearthed tangible evidence of the historical truth of King Minos and the associated legend of the Labyrinth.[2] Although inspired by Schliemann—and in many ways his interpretations of the site catered to his readings of the Greek myths—Evans never intended himself merely to be Crete's version of that great man; his goals were altogether loftier (Lapatin 2002:37–38), nothing less than uncovering the origins of Western civilization. His excavations, analyses, and interpretations of the site, plus its subsequent reconstruction, placed Crete on the archaeological map. Evans's was not the first archaeological work on the island. Greek archaeologists had been active prior to Evans's arrival. Minos Kolokairinos, a merchant and antiquarian living in Iraklio, was the original finder and excavator of Knossos, in 1878 (*Athena Review* 2003a; Hamilakis 2002a:2). He located the west magazines and twelve complete pithoi (Papadopoulos 2005:95). Joseph Hazzidakis was instrumental in founding both the Philekpaideftikos Syllogos (*Society of the Friends of Education*), which served as the island's informal department of antiquities, and also the Archaeological Museum in Iraklio (McEnroe 2002:65–66). He excavated at Gournes, Archalochori, Gaze, Anapolis, Nirou Khani, Tylissos, and Mallia (McEnroe 2002:66). Hazzidakis ceded the excavation rights to Mallia to the French School, because they had the finances (McEnroe 2002:66), and in fact, most early work was conducted by non-Greeks working through foreign schools simply because they had the necessary funds for large-scale excavation. However, all these figures were simply members of the supporting cast. Evans was the star of the show; he captured the preeminent position in Minoan archaeology and he never let it go. Even today, Evans's ghost haunts the halls of Minoan studies, just as his bronze bust dominates the entranceway to Knossos.[3]

As was typical of archaeology in the early twentieth century, emphasis was placed on excavating large, complex sites that would offer museum-quality artifacts as well as impressive architectural remains. This emphasis was stimulated not just by the need for visually attractive artifacts and architecture, but also by the well-founded assumption that large sites would offer the best chance of providing the stratigraphy necessary for chronology building. This goal is still important, for the island still does not have a universally accepted Bronze Age chronology, and indeed refining the chronology continues to exercise Minoan archaeologists.

Investigations today are conducted both by the Greek Archaeological Service and the numerous foreign schools permitted to work on the island. Excavations are still being conducted at the large sites. How-

Figure 2.2 *North entranceway to Knossos*

ever, the era of large-scale excavations seems to be drawing to a close in favor of survey projects (Rehak and Younger 2001:466) that focus more on surface identification and analysis of the total population of sites over wide areas of the island (cf. Kardulias [1994a:2] for the impact of this trend on Greek archaeology in general) and in favor of excavating the smaller sites that are invaluable in providing a more complete picture of Bronze Age life. Many of these projects are still research-oriented, but increasingly many digs are generated by the need to mitigate sites in the face of modern development projects. Although Renfrew (2003:313) has bemoaned the time lag between many surveys in Greece and the publication of their results, nevertheless the massive increase in available data from Aegean sites has been noted by numerous scholars (e.g., Broodbank 2004:46), to the point that even Aegean specialists have a hard time keeping up with them (Davis 2001:19). At the same time there is an increased commitment to what might be called anthropological archaeology, in which a wider range of interdisciplinary questions and techniques are formulated and employed (Watrous 2001).

Table 2.1

Generalized Minoan Chronology (after Hamilakis and Momigliano 2006)

Period	Years b.c. (circa)
Protopalatial (Old Palace)	**1950–1700**
Middle Minoan IB (MM IB)	1950–1900
Middle Minoan II (MM II)	1900–1700
Neopalatial (New Palace)	**1700–1430**
Middle Minoan III (MM III)	1700–1600
Late Minoan IA (LM IA)	1600–1510
Late Minoan IB (LM IB)	1510–1430
Final Palatial	**1430–1190**
Late Minoan II (LM II)	1430–1390
Late Minoan IIIA (LM IIIA)	1390–1330
Late Minoan IIIB (LM IIIB)	1330–1190

Despite the intensive work of the past hundred years or so, there is still no single established chronology for the Minoan Bronze Age (Cadogan 1992a:32; Dickinson 1994:10). Evans's was the first, and although it early on attracted criticism it has been hard to eradicate entirely (Papadopoulos 2005:105). Although this study is not primarily concerned with the substantive culture history of the island, the sites under consideration nevertheless must be placed into a broad temporal framework (Table 2.1).

Chronologies for Minoan Crete are variously based on correlations with Egyptian pottery (imported Minoan pottery has been found in Egyptian sites and Egyptian pieces found at Knossos), architectural styles, and radiocarbon dates. Evans's original nomenclature—Early, Middle, and Late Minoan—echoes that civilization's Old, Middle, and Late Kingdoms respectively. The building histories of the major palaces provide a complementary chronology: Prepalatial, Old Palace (Protopalatial), New Palace (Neopalatial), Postpalatial (Cadogan 1992a:32–33). Dickinson (1994:13) offers Prepalatial, First Palace, Second Palace, Third Palace, and Postpalatial periods.

Betancourt's (1987) "high chronology" amendment to the Late Minoan chronology would have the Late Minoan period beginning in 1700 rather than 1600 b.c. This revised chronology is based in part on dating the destruction of Akrotiri on Thera to the seventeenth century b.c. rather than a century later, but the revision has not yet been universally accepted (cf. Cullen 2001:9). The Early Minoan Period is traditionally seen as the precursor to the florescence of mature palace culture. The Middle Minoan period is marked by the appearance of the so-called palaces together with a centralized political and economic organization. Wheel-thrown pottery was introduced, along with writing. Population is thought to have increased in comparison to the preceding period (Davaras 1976:196). The Late Minoan period covers the florescence of Minoan culture. Around 1430 B.C. the island received heavy influence from the Mycenaeans, an influence that may have taken the form of a physical occupation.

In these chronologies two dates stand out. First, about 1700 B.C. the Old Palaces were destroyed by earthquake and rebuilt in the New Palace style. Macdonald (2003) refines this date, showing that although the Old Palace at Phaistos was destroyed at the end of MM IIB, the Old Palace at Knossos did not suffer the same amount of damage and it survived until it too was finally destroyed by a massive earthquake at the beginning of the seventeenth century. Most of what is visible at the palaces today belongs to the New Palace Period. At Knossos, Macdonald (2003) has further recognized three construction phases for the New Palace: the New Palace itself, the Frescoed Palace, the Ruined Palace (Appendix I). Second, around 1430 B.C. the palaces as well as other centers were destroyed by fire (either natural or human caused). Knossos was only partially destroyed at this time, finally succumbing to fire a few decades later.

The New Palace period saw economic and political stability in Crete, as evidenced by the construction of many large houses both in the country (e.g., Vathypetro), in the middle of towns (e.g., Gournia), and close to existing palaces (e.g., Knossos). Agricultural production during the New Palace Period was integrated with manufacturing and exporting various commodities (Sherratt and Sherratt 1991:369). Political and other forms of power may have been transferred between different polities for periods of time. For example, La Rosa (1997) has hypothesized that at some point during the New Palace Period, the bureaucratic and administrative center of the Mesara Plain, the largest and richest arable plain in the island, was transferred from Phaistos to nearby Agia Triada. It is unlikely, however, that Knossos was ever the *capital* of the island, at least as seen in centralized states like Egypt and Mesopotamia (Broodbank 2004:70).

After the second destruction of the palaces in the fifteenth century B.C., there is evidence for warfare, as seen in the burials of warriors with their weapons and in frescoes from Knossos that depict chariot scenes. Villas and settlements were abandoned by their inhabitants (Dickinson

1994:73), although where the inhabitants fled to is unclear. At Palaikastro, the drainage system was no longer maintained (Dickinson 1994:73).
It seems reasonable to conclude that after the palaces had lost their
power, some sort of social instability must have ensued, although the
depth of this is uncertain. There is some suggestion that political power
shifted to the west of the island, with the settlement at Chania surviving as a palatial center (Dickinson 1994:76) and actually becoming the
capital if not of the whole of the island then at least the western half.
Sherratt and Sherratt (1991:371) envisage Crete at this time as a series
of small polities, whose wealth depended on raw commodities like olive oil. During this period, the Mycenaean-controlled Knossian polity
exercised political and economic control over more than half of the island. Some models indicate that these social and political changes were
the result of a Mycenaean occupation of or infiltration into the island.
However, the term *occupation* is perhaps too suggestive of a physical
and military domination to be consistent with some of the archaeological evidence. As with many of the specifics of Minoan culture history,
further investigations need to be conducted.

Minoan Culture

Site Types

Investigations have revealed a wide range of Bronze Age archaeological
sites, reflective of the island's social and cultural complexity; many of
the sites were linked by roads (Rehak and Younger 2001:468). Site types
include palaces, villas, towns, sanctuaries, and tombs. This classifica-
tion system suffers from the same problem as all similar archaeological systems, namely that the terms are drawn from a modern Western
vocabulary. While this may be unavoidable, the loadedness of these
terms unfortunately brings with them connotations of function and
meaning that are often at odds with the evidence from the individual
sites themselves.

Palaces: The term *palace* was applied to Knossos by Kolokairinos,
Schliemann, and later Evans (Driessen 2003), who then applied associated terms like *throne room* and *piano nobile* for their specific architectural features. This nomenclature is unfortunate as it implies a primarily residential function reminiscent of the European palaces of the
nineteenth century, whereas they probably served a number of other

roles, such as administrative, religious, and political centers for large surrounding territories. Schoep (2002:33) points out that all our knowledge about the palaces is in flux and needs to be reevaluated. Each palace needs to be individually studied in terms of the type of power it wielded and also the geographical extent of that power.

The spatial plan of the palaces is organized around a central courtyard, their most important defining and characteristic feature (Miller 2003). The multi-story buildings surrounding the central courtyard housed residential, administrative, religious, and storage facilities. Specific architectural features include the Minoan hall (several rooms separated by a row of columns and a set of square piers [Hitchcock 2003]), lustral basins, pillar crypts, and light wells and the use of ashlar (cut) masonry with a rubble core (Davaras 1976:239-241).[4] Structural stability was enhanced by the use of wooden columns, pillars, and roof beams. Columns were made from inverted tree-trunks, both to prevent the green wood from resprouting and to prevent rainwater from running down their exterior. Many walls were covered in vividly painted frescoes, most of which are only fragmentary, resulting in rather speculative reconstructions in some instances (for example, at Knossos). Palaces also boasted extensive water systems, comprising both open stone channels and buried clay piping made up of sections up to 30 inches in length. The system brought fresh water into the buildings (often from rain cisterns located on the roofs) and took effluent away. The four most important sites (determined by their places in the academic and tourist hierarchies) are the palaces of Knossos, Phaistos, Mallia, and Kato Zakro. However, on the basis of the presence of a central court, Gournia, Galatas, and Petras could well be added to the list (Soles 2002; MacGillivray 2003; Tsipopoulou 2003). MacGillivray further notes that the sites at Chania (see also Andreadaki-Vlasaki 2002), Kommos, Archanes, Agia Triada, and Monistiraki, although lacking a central court, have palatial features like archives and fine architecture. Why the palaces appeared around 1900 B.C. is unclear. At one end of the range of explanations are those that see them as the result of long-standing trends that originated in the third millennium. At the other end are models that acknowledge such long-term factors as a growing population and increased foreign contact but suggest that the change over to the palace system was still relatively rapid.

The role of the palaces in the Minoan economy is still debated. On the one hand, using the numbers of pithoi and storage magazines found at them, Renfrew (1972) suggested that the palaces served as distribution centers for resources such as grain, olives, wine, and the like. Davaras (1976:252) estimated that the magazines at Knossos could have held as many as 400 pithoi with a combined storage volume of over 240,000 gallons. Smaller sites and settlements were part of a hierarchy built around the palace economy (cf. Haggis 2002:121–122). On the other hand, Sherratt and Sherratt (1991:366) have argued that the palaces were essentially exploitative, not redistributive, and vied to monopolize external trade (Sherratt and Sherratt 1991:365). Driessen (2003) has suggested that the palaces were primarily religious in nature. In his view, central courts were first built for ceremonial and ritual use about 2500 B.C. (based on recent excavations at Mallia) and that the buildings that today we call palaces were then built around the central courts in order to prevent outsiders from witnessing the rituals. Hitchcock (2003), too, sees the palaces as relying on religious belief and ritual to legitimize their economic activities. The courts may have served as the location of the bull games, although this conjecture is virtually impossible to prove. These games involved the acrobatic vaulting over bulls, as part of some ritual. They are represented on frescoes (for example, at Knossos) as well as on artifacts such as seals and vessels (for example, the stone Boxer rhyton from Agia Triada).

Rituals were shared by all the sites that had courts, as suggested by their common proportions (2:1) and orientations (slightly east of north). The court at Knossos is the largest and it has been calculated that it could have accommodated close to 5,500 individuals (about one quarter of the estimated population of greater Knossos). Court-centered buildings may have been built throughout the countryside "in imitation of Knossos to provide a setting for ritual performances that imitated those performed at Knossos itself" (Soles 2002:131). Until a clearer picture of the palaces and their social, political, religious, and economic roles emerges, the exact nature of their relationship to the surrounding countryside will remain largely elusive. Driessen et al. (2002) propose three broad hypotheses: (1) the palace was a seat of traditional central authority, with some form of hereditary kingship and a circumscribed territory; (2) Minoan society was a dynamic interplay of different factions with the winning faction residing in the palace; (3) real political power lay outside the palace, which was used as a ceremonial and religious center by different groups. Old palaces at Knossos, Phaistos, Mallia, and Kato Zakro may have controlled large territories—a possibility suggested by spatial heterogeneity in pottery styles—and served as economic, administrative, and possibly religious centers.

Villas: These structures had their roots in the pre-Palatial period (Niemeier 1997). They were an important feature of the Minoan-built landscape and they probably served as major players in local agricultural production, as evidenced at sites such as Vathypetro (with the remains of a wine and oil press) and Sklavokambos, and by the existence of satellite settlements around them (cf. Hamilakis 2002c:183). The term *villa* is ambiguous and membership in this category depends on possession of a number of topographical, architectural, and material culture features (van Effenterre and van Effenterre 1997). Betancourt and Marinatos (1997) identify three subtypes: (1) country villas standing alone in the countryside (very rare); (2) manorial villas that dominated a small village; (3) urban villas set in a city or suburbs. All three subtypes share such features as ashlar masonry, pier and door partition walls, pillar crypts, and adyta.

Towns: Concentration of the Minoan population into urban centers began in the second millennium. Some of these towns were associated with the palaces, which served as regional centers; unfortunately, as Davaras has noted (1976:333), excavations have concentrated on the palaces, so less is known about this particular settlement type. Indeed, it is not even clear how large the overall Cretan population was at this time; Rackham and Moody (1996:97) have suggested a population of anywhere from 216,000 to 271,000. A clearer picture emerges in the eastern part of the island where towns such as Gournia and Palaikastro have been excavated. These and others were built on small hills overlooking a good harbor. Towns boasted regular street plans with well-defined housing blocks. Palaikastro was laid out on a rectangular grid pattern (Davaras 1976:332). At Gournia (Figure 2.3), the streets radiate out from the small central palace, and these are further interconnected by concentric streets. Dickinson (1994:64) has gone so far as to identify possible suburbs at the town of Gournia separated by a natural dip in the ground surface. Presumably, these towns economically—and perhaps politically—controlled their own individual territories. No traces of city walls remain at these towns, with the exception of Petras (Dickinson 1994:65). The remains at these towns, as well as numerous frescoes and the so-called Town Mosaic from Knossos, indicate that the houses were several stories in height, with flat facades, and made of a variety of materials. Smaller villages and hamlets have been identified in both the Old and New Palace periods (Rackham and Moody 1996:89). Some towns performed specialized functions such as serving a harbor. Crete's coastline is relatively deficient in natural harbors, although ships could be dragged onto beaches if necessary. Simple harbor installations were built to facilitate the loading and unloading of ships. Shaw (2006:53–54)

Figure 2.3 *Gournia*

has identified two types of Bronze Age harbor. The first comprised land-ing areas on either side of a peninsula, on which was situated the associ-ated town. The second was found in an open and broad beach protected by an offshore islet. The harbor towns of Palaikastro and Kommos indi-cate the importance of maritime trade in the Minoan economy.

Sanctuaries: During the Middle Minoan period, some hilltops were converted into places of worship, often with a small built structure. Exca-vations at these so-called peak sanctuaries, of which at least twenty- five are known (Rackham and Moody 1996:179), have revealed thousands of votive offerings in the form of small clay animals as well as small clay anthropomorphs that represent the worshippers themselves, perhaps in some form of ecstatic body posture (Rackham and Moody 1996:107; Morris and Peatfield 2002:107). During the First Palace period these sanctuaries represented a rural nature cult, but by the following, Second Palace Period, they had been appropriated by the palace elites and their number had been reduced to those associated with palaces and towns (Morris and Peatfield 2002:108).

Evidence of cult worship dating back to the Neolithic is found in numerous caves on the island, perhaps the natural stalagmites and stalactites serving as cult images. Cave sanctuaries, of which at least nineteen are known (Rackham and Moody 1996:179), contain material culture remains interpreted as cult offerings. The cave at Arkalochori, for instance, contained swords and golden double axes. Other important cave sites include the Idaian cave and Kamares cave (both on Mount Psiloriti), and the Cave of Psychro (the Dictaian cave).

Tombs: Disposal of the dead was mostly though inhumation. The earliest cremations belong to the MM III period, but it became more prevalent in the LM III period (Davaras 1976:58). Inhumations were made in communal tholos tombs, built entirely aboveground, and perhaps serving as ossuaries. After 1450 B.C., there is a shift to the collective inhumation of smaller groups and even individuals in smaller tholos tombs or chamber tombs (*dromoi*) cut into the limestone (the site of Armeni, just south of Rethymno, is a good example of this style.) Bodies were placed in clay bathtub-shaped *larnakes* (probably their original function was as bathtubs.) All burials were communal although an individual could receive more attention through larnax burial or the addition of grave goods (Driessen 2002:5).

Economy

It is likely that most people owned or worked land, even those who also had specialist tasks such as craftsmen, priests, and administrators (Dickinson 1994:69). The subsistence economy was based on the cultivation of cereals and pulses, together with olives, figs, and vines. Emmer wheat appears to be the most important of the cereals, although barley and bread wheat were also cultivated (Davaras 1976:3; Dickinson 1994:45). Other exploited plants include almonds, beans, lentils, peas, pistachios, celery, garlic, lettuce, onions, and a variety of herbs and spices, such as thyme, basil, oregano, mint, sage, cumin, and marjoram (Davaras 1976:3; Dickinson 1994:47). Fruits include pears and apples (Davaras 1976:3). Carob and fig trees and date palms, probably imported from Egypt, may also have been grown (ibid). There is evidence of olive cultivation on Crete by the late Neolithic period, much earlier than on the mainland, where it was not important until the Late Bronze Age. Olive cultivation peaked on Crete in the Early Bronze Age (Moody 1997:68–70). Perhaps only the palaces were able to extensively cultivate the so-called orchard plants, olives, figs, and vines, because these plants produce in quantity only after many years of cultivation (Dickinson 1994:47). It is possible, following Renfrew (1972), that because cultivation of these plants did not use up land necessary for subsistence crop production, they served as exchange commodities (cf. Dickinson [1994:46] for alternative views to this hypothesis). Pigs, sheep, and goats were domesticated both for their meat and ancillary products. Cattle were less important as a food source, at least according to the Knossos texts (Dickinson 1994:40), and were used as draught animals. Horses and donkeys were used as beasts of burden. Bees were kept for honey. Both the domesticated dog and cat were present, as possibly were domestic fowl. Horses were probably introduced to the island sometime in the second millennium and were used to pull chariots (Dickinson 1994:144–145).

Surplus agricultural and other products, especially oil, wheat, barley, figs, and olives, were exchanged between the different palaces (Renfrew 1972:296–297) and presumably between the different communities on the island. Renfrew (1972:297) envisaged the palaces as redistributive centers of subsistence commodities controlled by a social hierarchy, rather reminiscent of the agricultural cooperatives found today on the island (Renfrew 1972:307). Indeed, for Renfrew centralized control of redistribution is the key to understanding the rise of Aegean civilization. Sherratt and Sherratt (1991:351) have argued against the palaces as market centers because such commodities were confined to the upper echelons of society and not marketed to the general population. Hamilakis (1996, 1999) has suggested that commodities were used by elites in large-scale communal feasting and drinking in order to consolidate and legitimize their power, to exploit labor, and to attract a retinue that could outcompete other groups of elites.

Long-distance trade was conducted by the Minoans throughout the Aegean, including Egypt and Sumeria (Renfrew 1972:455–460; Dickinson 1994:241–256). Exchange with islands to the north intensified after the construction of the Old Palaces (Davis 2001:25). Although Evans's original conception of a Minoan thalassocracy has been superseded, the existence of Minoan *colonies* on such islands as Kythera, Thera, Kea, Melos, and Rhodes, all of them importing large quantities of pottery (Renfrew 1972:367), suggests the mercantile and maritime power of the island during this period, as well as the aggrandizing qualities that local elites saw in Minoan culture. This process of *Minoanization* (Broodbank 2004:46) led to the adoption of Minoan items and behaviors beyond Crete: artifact styles, cooking habits, writing, weight systems, weaving, wall painting, burial practices, ritual action, and architectural styles. Imports from Egypt and the eastern Mediterranean, such as scarabs, beads, and amulets, were mostly channeled through Crete (Renfrew 1972:456). Copper was imported from Cyprus (Davaras 1976:195). Laconia provided semiprecious stones. Gold came in from Nubia and silver from Anatolia (Sherratt and Sherratt 1991:361). One of Minoan Crete's most important exports was wool; tablets at Knossos record a total number of 100,000 sheep (Davaras 1976:54). Cretan wool cloth was highly prized in Egypt (Sherratt and Sherratt 1991:359). Olive oil was also an important export (Davaras 1976:212), and sixteenth century B.C. stirrup jars were the first standardized liquid transport containers (Sherratt and Sherratt 1991:363). Other exports included timber, wine and honey, and resin. The Minoan trading fleet must have played an important role in sea trade. Ships of that time relied heavily on oars not just to overcome calm weather but also to counter contrary winds, as their square sails were not particularly good at sailing into the wind. Inbound and outbound routes were consequently different from each other in order to accommodate winds and currents (Sherratt and Sherratt 1991:357). The importance of long-distance trade may lie not so much in the absolute quantities of materials moved—in fact, these quantities were relatively small, and there are no storage facilities comparable to those found in Mesopotamian states—but in their stimulating local surpluses that could then be fed into the exchange system (Sherratt and Sherratt 1991:354). Yet, it is still difficult to estimate precisely the importance of trade in the overall development of Cretan Bronze Age civilization (cf. Sherratt and Sherratt 1991:351).

Social and Political Structure

Debates on political and social dynamics in Bronze Age Crete are still influenced by the stereotypes which portray Minoan Crete as a high European civilization with strong hierarchical structures, kings and aristocracy. —Hamilakis (1998:233)

. . . we should bury "King Minos." —Driessen (2002:13)

Minoan society was almost certainly ranked, for it is surely inconceivable that building projects the size of Knossos or indeed the other palaces could have been completed without some sort of centralized control. Moreover, there is evidence for diversity in grave goods at sites like Mochlos. Social ranking would have been fostered if there had been an agricultural surplus and/or differential wealth, resulting perhaps from foreign trade (cf. Hitchcock 2003). Ranking need not have been organized along a Marxist class model (i.e., bourgeois/proletariat); however, the specifics of Minoan social organization still need to be adequately addressed (Hamilakis 2002a:4). Renfrew (1972:364–365) suggested that Minoan social structure was similar to that of a chiefdom, characterized by a chief who existed at the top of a hierarchy based on individual personal ranking. He proposed a class society, though not one based strictly on economic status: "the society is . . . graded internally, like a feudal aristocratic class, but with no mass of peasants underneath." Hamilakis (2002c) saw the social hierarchy as an extremely fluid and fragile political organization based on competing factions.

It is still unclear if any one individual controlled Minoan society. Evans's original conclusion, which held sway until the 1980s, was that Knossos, at least by the Neopalatial period, controlled the island as the head of a single unified state, or at the very least as a confederation of city-states (cf. Davaras 1976:2; Driessen and Macdonald 1997), based on the homogeneity of material culture and the prevalence of Linear A tablets in sites throughout the island (Driessen 2003). Evans's conceptualization of the monarchy as held by a priest-king inadvertently helped avoid the debate of what power in the palaces was actually constituted in: politics, economics, religion, or a combination. Betancourt (2002:211)—relying on the evidence for trade and metallurgy, palace architecture, the establishment of peace, and the storage and control of commodities—has argued that the "evidence indicates that the Cretan palaces had a strong direction, and the most likely situation requires a central political leader, which we would call a king." Certainly, the monumentality of the palaces must have inspired onlookers, but was this inspiration political, economic, or religious in nature, or a combination of all three? Driessen (2003) and MacGillivray (2003) point out that it is highly unlikely that Minoan society was run by a hereditary monarchy, and there is no evidence at Knossos or elsewhere on Crete for a monarchy until the *wanax* (the head of a Mycenaean city-state) of the Mycenaean archives (MacGillivray 2002:213). The throne room at Knossos was not Minoan, but rather dates to the period of Mycenaean occupation, when a mainland *wanax* controlled Knossos. There are no iconographic representations of individual rulers, nor does the layout of Knossos lead one to a central throne complex, both of which are common features in ancient states with a hereditary ruler. No burials could be conceivably interpreted as royal (Driessen 2002:5), though Betancourt (2002:207) would not agree. Driessen (2002:3), in particular, has emphasized the religious nature of power in Knossian society and that art may have served as propaganda of a religious and cult nature, rather than that of a secular ruler. He concedes that the throne room at Knossos is dated to the Mycenaean period, but that even if it did have political significance it had religious significance as well (Driessen 2002:3).

Variety in site size and function is suggestive of some sort of political and/or economic hierarchy. Not only has it proven difficult to confirm the actual number of palaces on the island, however, but the internal hierarchy of these sites is still unclear. A settlement hierarchy has been provided by Warren (2002:201): central palaces or capitals; towns/villages/ports; hamlets; small farms/estates/villas. However, as excavations at more and more sites have shown their own palatial features, and the adequacy of excavation data is questioned (cf. Hamilakis 2002c:185), the model may prove to have been offered prematurely. McGillivray (1997) has argued for attempts by Knossos to exert a local hegemony as early as the Old Palace period. While Knossos *may* have controlled the central portion of the island by the New Palace period, elsewhere local elite groups independently ran their own territories (Driessen and Macdonald 1997; Driessen 2003). For example, the palace of Petras may have controlled the whole of the Siteia basin (Tsipopoulou 2002, 2003). We, thus, have three possible models: (1) Knossian hegemony; (2) palaces existing as independent units; (3) palaces operating as independent units but with an ideological allegiance to Knossos (Schoep 2002:15–16).

Also now largely abandoned is Evans's portrayal of the *Pax* Minoica (MacGillivray 2000), with pacific, well-off, and tolerant Minoans, safe behind the wooden walls of their navy, much the same way as he saw Victorian England. This view was the norm until quite recently when excavations showed that the Minoans did build defensive walls, at least from the Protopalatial period, based on the evidence from Petras (Tsipopoulou 2003). Walls are found at Gournia, Mallia, and Petras, although their not completing a full circle can call into question their actual function. Stylianos Alexiou and Stella Chryssoulaki both have observed Minoan military architecture, the latter suggesting that a series of forts controlled the Minoan countryside (MacGillivray 2000:312). Evans apparently knew about these but preferred to ignore them (ibid).

Art and Technology

The magnificence of Minoan art has long been noted, whether it be the frescoes at Knossos and elsewhere or the individual pieces rendered in such media as pottery, precious metals, stone, and faience (Biers 1996:29–61). These artworks have been celebrated since their discovery for their vitality and originality. They dominate the majority of the material on display in the Iraklio Museum as well as in the smaller museums throughout the island. Unfortunately, especially in regard to the so-called snake goddess figurines, not all of them may be original, some of them having being produced at the time Knossos was being excavated, to supply a profitable illicit trade (cf. Lapatin [2002] and Papadopoulos [2005:134] for more on this practice). Early Minoan pottery was hand-formed. A variety of vessel shapes and sizes were made, of various styles. Vasiliki Ware is a high-quality red-brown mottled ware. The succeeding middle Minoan period saw the introduction of the potter's wheel. The polychrome Kamares Ware, which dates to MM I and MM II (the Old Palace period), is beautifully designed with a variety of external decorative motifs. It was exported as far afield as Egypt, Syria, and Cyprus. Naturalism is seen in the Floral Style and Marine Style pottery of the LM I period. The Palace Style (LM II), at first confined to the Knossos area, dates to LM II (1450–1400 B.C.) and also showed a naturalistic style. The Mycenaean occupation of the island led to an increase in the manufacture of a standardized style of pottery; the pottery is nevertheless of a very high technical quality. The Minoans also worked in organic materials like bone and ivory (the latter imported) and metallurgy to make objects both utilitarian and aesthetic. A particularly famous piece is the much-reconstructed ivory acrobat figurine from Knossos (now in the Iraklio Museum). The multi-colored frescoes date to the Neopalatial period. Most of them come from Knossos and Agia Triada, with smaller sets found at Amnisos and Tylissos (Dartmouth.edu 1997a). At Knossos, the most common themes on the frescoes are (1) bull leaping and catching, (2) boxing and wrestling, (3) heraldic griffins, and (4) processional scenes. Scenes of hunting and warfare are absent (ibid).

Writing Systems

Minoan Crete developed three writing systems (Bennet 2000). The earlier two of the three, Cretan hieroglyphics and Linear A, are still undeciphered. Cretan hieroglyphics on sealstones and clay tablets were in use as early as 1900 B.C. (*Athena Review* 2003b). The famous Phaistos disk (made of clay, some six inches in diameter, and found at the site of the same name) dates to the seventeenth century B.C. It contains a series of 242 hieroglyphs, arranged in sixty-one groups that begin on the outer edge and spiral their way into the center. Linear A takes its name from the characteristic use of strokes or lines and appears to have developed between 1850 and 1700 B.C. It was not a written form of early Greek. Pa-padopoulos (2005:131) has suggested that it might be related to Luwian, an Indo-European language spoken in southern Anatolia. The script is found at a number of sites throughout the island and as far away as Santorini and Samothrace. Linear A was used mainly for commercial recording, with ideograms representing livestock and other commodities (Dickinson 1994:193). The third system, Linear B, deciphered by Michael Ventris in the 1950s, appears to be a Greek-language version of Linear A, resulting from the heavy contact with the island by mainland Greeks in the mid-fifteen century B.C., who then adopted Linear A to their own language (a good synthesis of Linear B studies is provided by Palaima [2003]). Linear B, like Linear A, is a syllabary and, again like its predecessor, was used primarily for the recording of inventories, military supplies, and withdrawals or deposits from the palace stores (Biers 1996:26). The names of Minoan sites like Knossos and Amnisos have been found on Linear B tablets (*Athena Review* 2003a). It is likely that the scribes formed a specialized professional class within Minoan society, and the fact that writing was essentially limited to an administrative function suggests that it was not widespread. It disappeared when the palace economy collapsed (Davaras 1976:184).

Religion

Religion appears to have been a pervasive element in Minoan society (Peatfield 2000:138), although its specific organization and development are still debated. Sanctuaries were excavated during the early part of the twentieth century, but they were overshadowed by the treasures coming out of the palaces (Peatfield 2000:47). In assigning religious terminology to many rooms and artifacts in Knossos, Evans perhaps did the study a disservice in drawing attention away from an understanding of the context of religious activity and more to the physical remains of worship, a deficiency that modern studies are rectifying. Enacted and visionary epiphanies are seen as important elements in Minoan religion by Goodison and Morris (1999:128). Archaeological evidence for religious and ritual behavior includes (1) the locations of cult activity; (2) representations of these activities on items like seals, rings, murals, larnakes, and pottery; (3) cult furniture such as figurines, horns of consecration, and double axes; and (4) folk memories preserved in later Greek myth and ritual (Dartmouth.edu 1997b). Recent studies of peak sanctuaries by Peatfield (2000:148) have provided information on *nonelite* Minoan religious practices. Doorways of Mesara tombs almost all face eastward, perhaps connected to sunrise (Goodison and Morris 1999:117).

The so-called mother goddess was originally proposed by Evans as the most important figure in Minoan religion (Goodison and Morris 1999:113) and was associated by him with various elements of the natural environment and with animals, birds, and snakes (Peatfield 2000:139–140). Her best known representation is the snake goddess figurines, again first found by Evans at Knossos, which were deliberately and permanently buried in cists under the floor of the New Palace (Goodison and Morris 1999:123–124). Bulls, snakes, and doves figure in religious scenes. The bull was sacrificed, perhaps by the double axe, an important icon in Minoan religion (ibid). There is a possible shift at the beginning of the second millennium b.c. to more anthropomorphic and fewer zoomorphic and natural forms. Whether Minoan religion was monotheistic or polytheistic is still unclear (Nilsson 1950; Peatfield 2000:141). Polytheism is perhaps identified in the animistic and totemic nature of Minoan religion, although without the relevant texts such conclusions are speculative. The existence of a Minoan polytheism is tentatively supported by the still murky relationship of Minoan religion to the later Greek pantheon. Linear B tablets from Knossos list a number of Olympian deities together with Minoan deities as the recipients of the offerings (Goodison and Morris 1999:131; Peatfield 2000:141–142). Voyatzis (1999) has also discussed the connection between Bronze Age and later goddesses.

Recently, provocative, albeit controversial, indications of human cannibalism have come to light. The site of Anemospilia was destroyed at the end of MM II by fire, probably caused by the same earthquake that had destroyed the Old Palaces at Knossos and Phaistos. At this site three skeletons were recovered indicating, to some at least, ritual activity. The first skeleton was of an eighteen-year-old male who had possibly been trussed. It has been suggested that the so-called victim had been bled before death. Second, in the basement of the so-called *North House* (northwest of the Little Palace at Knossos) in a LM 1B context were found 327 children's bones, perhaps belonging to as few as four children (Dartmouth.edu 1997b). Some of the bones had cut marks suggestive of cannibalistic activity. In the same site complex a pithos was found containing human bones along with sheep bones. A quern stone with pounded bone was recovered from Keminospelio, and burnt human bones and a cooking pot containing a child's skeletal remains were found at Vorou (Hamilakis 2002d:128). The Mesara tombs have evidence of bones being cut, moved, and even removed, perhaps indicative of an ancestor cult (Goodison and Morris 1999:117).

Concluding Summary

These are, indeed, interesting times for Minoan archaeology. Despite over one hundred years of intensive excavation and survey, the essentially prehistoric nature of the evidence has left archaeologists still searching for answers to most of the fundamental questions about Minoan society. Moreover, a new revisionist trend has scholars questioning just about every interpretation that has gone before. Remarkably, however, the uncertainty of contemporary Minoan archaeology is not translated into what is offered to the public. The public, despite the diversity in the sources of the different media, is presented with a dated yet remarkably coherent and homogeneous narrative. The intent of Chapter 4 is to pursue this line of thought by isolating what is told and what is not told to the public at archaeological sites on the island and through the various media of information that they typically use. However, first we must examine in a little more depth what exactly is meant by the word *tourist*. This is the purpose of the next chapter.

NOTES

1. Kotsakis (1991), for example, notes the fact that Greek prehistoric archaeology has tended to lag behind contemporary theoretical developments. Morris (1994:15) has called Greek Bronze Age prehistory the "soft underbelly of Hellenism." Most recently, Renfrew (2003:315) has bemoaned the continuing lack of comparative studies. Like other areas, Aegean archaeology has its own authority structure in which certain discourses are allowed and others closed down. Preziosi (personal communication, cited in Hitchcock and Koudounaris [2002:43]) has put it very bluntly in his reference to "the very palpable authority-structure and socialization protocols in Aegean archaeology, whereby one is programmed very specifically into not raising questions or issues which might call into question the unassailability of a given scholar's pronouncements."

2. In this legend, Knossos was ruled by King Minos, who kept imprisoned in the underground labyrinth, built for him by the master craftsman Daedalus, a monster, the Minotaur, a half-man, half-bull, product of an illicit union between Minos's wife, Pasiphae, and a white bull. Theseus, the *prince* of Athens, was brought to Knossos with others to be fed to the Minotaur as part of an annual tribute from Athens of seven maidens and seven young men. Ariadne, Minos's daughter, fell in love with Theseus and provided him with a sword with which to slay the Minotaur and with a ball of twine which he used to retrace his path out of the labyrinth. Theseus succeeded in killing the monster and sailed back to Athens where he assumed the throne, hav-

ing first abandoned Ariadne on Naxos. Evans's research, alongside that of others, does provide support for this story as at least a metaphor for real historical events: for instance, the rumbling of the captive Minotaur echoes the seismic disturbances that regularly wrack Crete; the labyrinth is really the palace of Knossos with its twisting corridors; Theseus is a mainland invader who in slaying the Minotaur destroys the military and religious power of the Minoan ruling class. The best version of this story is still Mary Renault's (1958) classic *The King Must Die*.

3. I was fortunate to be invited to participate in the 2005 Venice symposium on the construction of the Minoan past (Hamilakis and Momigliano 2006). I was struck by how amongst these very forward-looking scholars Evans and his work were never far distant.

4. Lustral basins are small rectangular rooms below floor level. They are often lined with gypsum and are entered by a short flight of stairs. They were originally named by Evans, who conceived them as places for ritual purification through bathing. This interpretation has been questioned, given that gypsum dissolves in water, that the basins have no drains, that they are overly deep for bathing, and in the case of one at Knossos that they are situated where their users were potentially in full view (Hitchcock 2003). Davaras (1976:189) has suggested that only a very small amount of water was used, perhaps merely to sprinkle the participants.

Tourists and the Constructed Past

Modern tourism has its roots in the eighteenth century with the Grand Tour (Nash 1981:462; Cohen 1995:12), a prolonged stay in the cultural capitals of Europe—primarily in Italy—that gave wealthy young men from western Europe the level of cultural sophistication needed for them to take their rightful place in society (i.e., at the top). So-called *mass tourism*, in which touring was extended beyond a small elite of society, was allowed by the spread of industrial capitalism (Böröcz 1992:735–736), as more and more members of society, primarily the middle classes, gained sufficient leisure money to indulge themselves in trips elsewhere.[1] Travel for its own sake became increasingly a "bourgeois experience [with] its origins in the conjunction of romanticism and industrialism" (Duncan and Gregory 1999:6).

What precisely constitutes a tourist (and by extension tourism itself) is problematic, for the terms can be applied to a great variety of experiences, both domestic and foreign (Cohen 1974:527; MacCannell 1976:1; Nash 1981:464, 1996:168; Crick 1989:312; Smith 1989:1; Boissevain 1996:2–3), and it is worth keeping in mind MacCannell's (1976:1) reminder that tourists are actually real people and not just sociological subjects. Cohen (1974:531–532) defines tourists as travelers who are (1) temporary, (2) voluntary, (3) on a round-trip visit, (4) engaging in a relatively long journey, (5) on a nonrecurrent or rare visit, (6) and on a noninstrumental journey (i.e., the trip is not a means to an end but rather an end in itself). The end itself includes such goals as education and pilgrimage, visiting the old country or enjoying a different natural and cultural environment (Cohen 1974:542; Smith 1989:4–6). He further offers (Cohen 1974:541–543) thermalists, students, pilgrims, old-country visitors, conventioneers, business travelers, tourist-employees. Wickens (1994:819) categorizes tourists as cultural heritage types, ravers, Shirley Valentine, heliolatrous, Lord Byron. Dann and Cohen (1996:309), reflecting a *Weberian* approach, separate those who work at tourism, guidebook in hand in search of authenticity, from those who go for fun with no motive other than ludic enjoyment.

Despite this variability there are some commonalities that constitute what Nash and Smith (1991:14) have called the touristic process. This process originates with the decision to go to another country. It involves the actual journey itself and the encounter with another culture, diluted though that contact may be, and ends with the give-and-take between the host community and the tourist and with what the tourist takes away from the encounter. We can view the overall touristic process as one of separation, liminality, and reintegration. It is a period of separation in that the tourist is separated to some degree from his or her own culture. Some tour operators make an attempt to limit this sense of separation, whilst others actively market the trip as a new cultural experience. The trip abroad provides an opportunity for leisure (Nash and Smith 1991:14) and a "freedom from primary obligations" (Nash 1981:462). It is a period of liminality (Akeroyd 1981:468) in that the tourist is sanctioned to display behavior that would be unacceptable in his own society. It can also be seen as a pilgrimage (Cohen 1974; Burns 1999), a sacred journey from which the tourist, as part of the reintegration into his or her own culture, brings back souvenirs, objects to remind the returned tourist of the "myth sought on the journey . . . the memories of experiences" (Graburn 1989:33). The tourist is exposed to a controlled experience of a new cultural environment and may be expected to bring something back, physical and perhaps even spiritual. Plus, the tourist is part of what the operators intend to be a profitable enterprise. How these observations inform our understanding of the tourist's visit to an archaeological site or museum is the purpose of the rest of this chapter, which will examine the issues of authenticity and the commodification of the past.

The type of tourist I am particularly interested in for the purposes of this study has the following profile. This tourist has come to the island for something other than its archaeology. Probably he or she is there for sun, relaxation, and a change of environment. The tourist's knowledge of Knossos and the island's past has been gained primarily, if not exclusively, through nonacademic sources. He or she visits the site because it is touted as one of the island's premier attractions and perhaps because a site visit is included in the holiday package that has been paid for. There may never be a return visit to Crete and if there is it may not include a revisit to Knossos or other sites and museums. I would suspect that most of the visitors to Knossos fit this tourist profile.

The Dissolution of Authenticity

The ability of industrial technology to get tourists to "the exotic" meant that the exotic became mundane. Now exoticism continually had to be invented, and this pressure for the exotic continues today, as a glance through the travel section of any Sunday newspaper will confirm. Tourists continually seek out the exotic. However, this exoticism is not unalloyed, for it must be presented in a strictly controlled environment so that the tourist never feels totally lost. Indeed, a primary goal of the experience is to provide the visitor with a safe and familiar home environment combined with a controlled access to the outside. Getting the right balance is important. Tourist brochures emphasize not just the wonders of their foreign experience but also the luxury of the accommodation that the tourist will come home to at the end of a day of exotic visits (Bruner 2005:13-14).[2]

Although the tourist is attracted by the exotic nature of the chosen destination, what does he or she really experience of the host culture? This question compels an examination of the thorny issue of authenticity. This issue goes to the heart of the tourist experience because it asks whether the tourist in any way encounters genuine acts of cultural behavior on the part of the host community (Chambers 2000:98). Authentic experiences might include traditional Greek dances, Greek meals, or visits to Greek archaeological sites. Cohen (1988:383) has suggested that life for alienated moderns is inauthentic, and therefore they search out real or authentic experiences when they visit another country in order to acquire an antidote to the alienation the middle classes routinely feel during work activities (cf. MacCannell 1976). Authenticity is especially sought after by so-called elite tourists (Graburn and Moore 1994:236). Cohen (1988) argued that educational level correlates strongly with concerns for authenticity and that different tourists will have different definitions of what is authentic and what isn't. Some tourists, particularly well-educated professionals, might see through any inauthenticity; "Intellectuals, here exemplified by curators, ethnographers, and anthropologists, will generally be more alienated, and more aware of their alienation, than the rank-and-file middle classes, and especially the lower middle class, who still strive to attain the material gains which those already beyond them enjoy" (Cohen 1988:376). Perhaps some will identify inauthenticity merely in order to see through it and thereby demonstrate their cleverness. Graburn and Moore (1994:235) go so far as to ask whether middle-class researchers can even understand working-class tourists.

For other scholars, the result of any touristic interaction with a foreign culture, even if that interaction is intended to be an authentic experience, is a staged experience at best and an inauthentic one at worst. Certainly, Bruner's (2005:72) phrase "the questioning gaze" (a gentle play on Urry's phrase) recognizes the possibility that some tourists at least can be skeptical of what is being presented to them. Bruner (2005:3) has further observed that even up-scale groups are not necessarily interested in authenticity; they just want a good show. Is the tourist even concerned with—let alone able to see through—the inauthenticity of last night's traditional Greek dancer serving him breakfast the next morning in modern Western clothes? Perhaps others will accept the experience as authentic in a playful mode even if deep down they suspect it isn't; it is a ludic attitude (Cohen 1995:25), taken reflectively, not unwillingly. Most tourists are at play, which is a mixture of reality and make-believe (Cohen 1988:383), and mass tourism succeeds, not because it grossly misleads the tourist but partly because the average tourist has a different standard of authenticity than the professional observer. Crick (1985) has noted the difference between the scientific knowledge of the anthropologist and the knowledge acquired by the tourist. MacCannell (1973) has suggested that so-called authentic experiences are only *staged*, allowing the tourist to see only the front, as it were, of the host culture, rather being allowed in to see its inner workings. This staged authenticity can thwart the tourist's desire for authentic experiences and leads to a "false touristic consciousness" (Cohen 1988:373).

Perhaps, however, there is no essential distinction between authenticity and inauthenticity. Certainly, what was once inauthentic can become authentic through time (Cohen 1988:380; Kelleher 2004); witness how Disneyland has become part of an authentic American experience. Wolf (1982) first made explicit the problems of cultural authenticity and others, like Hobsbawm and Ranger (1983) and Anderson (1983), followed his lead. Authenticity implies an ability to isolate what is traditional (i.e., right) from what isn't. However, this is not objectively possible: "[w]hat is traditional in a culture is largely a matter of internal polemic as groups within a society struggle for hegemony, and a matter of external judgment when the anthropologist constitutes a particular image of a culture as its 'true' form" (Greenwood 1989:183). If all culture is staged to some extent (Crick 1989:336), and "if [cultural] change is a permanent state, why should the staging bound up in tourism be regarded as so destructive, and why should the changes be seen in such a negative light?" (Crick 1989:336). Authenticity in this perspective becomes a red herring (Bruner 2005:5) not worth the effort of capture[3] and the distinction between inauthenticity and authenticity, staged or otherwise, as unnecessary. This insight allows us to view the tourist visit to an archaeological site in a new light.

How, then, is the archaeological site or the museum part of the touristic process? First, most tourists visiting an archaeological site accept at face value what is on offer. I will play safe and exclude from this statement such professionals as anthropologists and other social scientists who might well have "more rigorous criteria of authenticity than do ordinary members of the traveling public . . . indeed, their alienation from modernity often induces them to choose their respective professions" (Cohen 1988:375–376). Even those who might question what they see will do so within a frame of reference provided by the site itself; in other words, they react to what is on offer rather than create something entirely new for themselves. While we might not want to go so far as to dissolve entirely the boundary between the authentic and the inauthentic in the encounter with a living culture, we are on surer ground in doing so when the tourist comes face-to-face with the past for the simple reason that the whole of the past is constructed in the present by people unrelated to it. What we see at the site (the dance, to use the former example as an analogy) is not performed by the people of the past for that would be an impossibility. The site is a performance presented by people in the present, that is, the archaeologists, site managers, and so forth. So when tourists visit a site, they are looking not just at the past but also at themselves, or at least at their society as defined by the people putting on the show. And it is this fact that makes the messages about that past so powerful in their impact on the present because it all seems so natural, so obvious. Moreover, because the site is portrayed as a laboratory where the truths of the past are uncovered (this is even more so for the visitors to museums, the scientific authority of which is even more omnipresent and palpable), the issue of (in)authenticity scarcely raises its head, except, as we shall see, in the case of Knossos. The scientific authority that therefore permeates these sites and museums denies the public a clear opportunity to recognize the political and ideological dimensions to the construction of the past. I would further argue that the dissolution of the boundary between authenticity and inauthenticity at a site and the fact that most tourists are there just for the show undermine the need to delineate the specific educational and socioeconomic status of tourists to sites.

The Commodified Past

Archaeological sites have been used as attractions since the beginnings of modern tourism (Cohen 1995:19) and have acquired a tangible value in the capitalist economy. Selling an archaeological site to the public is an act of commodification, which refers to the assigning of use- or exchange-value to a particular object that previously was outside the market system (Chambers 2000:94), a process that "lies at the complex intersection of temporal, cultural, and social factors" (Appadurai 1986:15). Like other commodities, a site acquires "a particular type of social potential" (Appadurai 1986:6), and in the case discussed here one manifestation of this new social potential is economic value. Appadurai (1986:4) follows Simmel (1978) and argues that "demand . . . endows the object with value." However, this order is reversed in the case of archaeological sites. They are first endowed with a value, which in the case of sites and museums on Crete is determined by noneconomic factors such as their importance in academic studies or their role in establishing a sense of Western identity. Only after their value has been established are the sites introduced into the market as a commodity. At this point the archaeological site ceases to exist as just a reliquary of the past and is imbued with all sorts of new contemporary values; it becomes fetishized (Marx 1986 [original 1867]:163) and is metamorphosed into something new (Appadurai [1986:16]).

As the importance of the past in promoting economic development has grown, more and more control of what is said and done with the past has been wrested from local communities. For example, tension continues between the inhabitants of the "old town" in Rethymno wishing to alter the exterior of their houses and the heritage bureaucrats in Athens whose mandate is the quarter's preservation as a piece of living history (Hertzfeld 1991). Similar conflicts have emerged in the village of Palaia Epidhavros on the Greek mainland as control of tourism development has shifted from the local inhabitants to the national government (Williams and Papamichael 1995). Boissevain (1996:7) notes that tourist organizations usually market culture without consulting the inhabitants, and this would appear to be the case on Crete, where locals must continuously contest their access to the past of their own island, a past that is largely defined by academics, government bureaucrats, and the tourist industry. Locals are separated from the creation of this past even as the Greek National Tourist Organization (GNTO) sells the Minoan past as the origins of Western culture (including presumably, that of contemporary Cretans themselves).

The increasing value of archaeological sites to tourism has resulted in more and more attention being paid to attendance figures and revenue expectation and less on scholarly knowledge (cf. Silberman 1995:261). In order to maximize its profit, the site and its past must be presented to the public in such a way as to ensure that the visitor, who is potentially a "genuine stranger" (Nash 1996:154), is comfortable with what he or she sees and learns—another example of the sought-after balance between the exotic and the familiar. Kristiansen (1992:9) refers to "the 'domestication' and 'cultivation' of history which makes it accessible to the present." It has been suggested elsewhere (Duke and Wilson 1995:10–11) that no archaeologist feels real culture shock on an archaeological site, because archaeologists create the past in terms that are intuitively understandable to them in the present, and this is similar to what the visitor to a site feels too. Lowenthal (1985) may be right in calling the past a foreign country, but this doesn't mean that it has to be strange. Indeed, as I noted earlier, archaeologists colonize it and populate it with figures familiar to them. The tourist industry then populates the colony with another wave of immigrants. Crick's (1989:328) observation that "[t]ourism is very much about *our* culture, not about *their* culture or our desire to learn about it" can very much be applied to the visitor experience at an archaeological site, too. Again, Lowenthal (1985:348):

> The past is always altered for motives that reflect modern needs. We reshape our heritage to make it attractive in modern terms; we seek to make it part of ourselves, and ourselves part of it; we conform it to our self-images and aspirations. Rendered grand or homely, magnified or tarnished, history is continually altered in our private interests or on behalf of our community or country.

The past becomes cultural reproduction. It reflects our present.

Archaeological sites, and to a lesser extent museums, which possess a more overtly educational and scientific character, must appeal to as many visitors as possible; otherwise there is little point to the sites' and the museum objects' being made accessible to the public in the first place. Thus, the past *de facto* becomes diluted and softened in order to ensure that as wide a range of visitors as possible are made to feel comfortable and thus willing to enter into it. The result is that the potential for the site to serve as a locus of discourse is minimized if not entirely obliterated. The past can potentially be threatening to structures of hegemony; it is one arena where our imagination can potentially be free, without the dictates and impositions of the present. And just as, follow-ing Habermas (1973), class struggle is mitigated by being displaced into state bureaucracy, so too does the past lose its potency for exposing al-ternative social arrangements by that very same displacement; dissent is institutionalized, and thereby marginalized. The past is further sani-tized in the sense of being cleaned up for public consumption. There is no accounting, to foreshadow the following chapter, of "the other side" of Bronze Age life, the undoubted disease and squalor and so on (cf. Lowenthal 1985:341). The past is not allowed to suggest other ways of living or other social arrangements. However, in sanitizing the past we perforce selectively leave out elements of that past. And these silences become as important as the voices that are allowed to be heard.

Apostolakis and Jaffry (2005) recently conducted an economic anal-ysis of what would make Knossos and the Iraklio Museum more at-tractive to tourists. Emphasis was placed on providing amenities such as restaurants and audiovisual equipment, and whether the sites were well advertised in their home countries. Respondents to their survey asked for a broader context (p. 241) for understanding the two sites, but no specificity for what this might mean was provided. This emphasis on the means of delivery rather than the contents of the message itself fits well with how the past has been co-opted by the tourist industry.

Summary

This chapter has initiated the exploration of the nexus between the tourist and the past as mediated by visits to archaeological sites and museums. It has argued that the past is contemporary cultural pro-duction. Because of this, any essential difference between authentic and inauthentic is dissolved and the tourist, faced with an entertaining show masquerading as a scientific presentation, accepts what is on offer. However, if the past is not solely scientifically constituted at sites and museums but rather is the product of other factors, then these other fac-tors must be specified if we are fully to understand the nexus. Chapter 4 examines the specific version of the Minoan past offered to the visitor both in what is said and what is left silent, and how the mechanisms by which that past is offered are ultimately so convincing.

NOTES

1. See Crick (1989), Honey (1999:7–10), and Chambers (2000) for brief histories of tourism, and Burns (1999:82–83) for some of the major players in tourism studies.
2. My experiences leading groups to Greece is that the right balance must be sought in the accommodation especially. Although participants expect some cultural differences, the hotels must provide the right *American* features (spacious rooms, hot and powerful showers, and so forth).
3. Yet some chilling exceptions remain, such as how the "Alarde" ritual practiced by the villagers of Fuenterrabia has been destroyed by its being turned into a public display for tourists (Greenwood 1989).

CHAPTER FOUR

Modern Crete, Ancient Minoans, and the Tourist Experience

Lord Jesus Christ, Son of God, have mercy on the cities, the islands and the villages of this Orthodox Fatherland, as well as the holy monasteries which are scourged by the worldly touristic wave. Grace with us a solution to this dramatic problem and protect our brethren who are so sorely tried by the modernistic spirit of these contemporary Western invaders.[1]

This chapter turns to the specific encounter of tourists with a Minoan past. It demonstrates the particular past articulated through a variety of media, as well as with but not limited to sites and museums. Through these media, the tourist is drawn into the myth of the past so that authenticity and inauthenticity are dissolved. At the same time the past is presented as one supported by scientific knowledge. The balance between science and myth results in a powerful and irresistible version of the Minoan past. It might first be useful, however, to contextualize these arguments by looking at some elements of the broader phenomenon of tourism on Crete.

Crete deserves its popularity as a tourist destination because it provides the visitor with a mix of a somewhat familiar culture spiced with the exotic (strangeness). The blending of the familiar and the exotic is in many ways an integral part of Cretan culture itself.[2] Certainly, past relations between the island and foreign visitors of all sorts reveal a deep-seated physical and cultural assonance.[3] The great Hellenophile, Lawrence Durrell (1978:58), for example, recognized a tension, something ominous, lurking not far beneath the surface of Crete: "[t]hough beautiful in its spacious style, its ruggedness and its sudden changes of weather make it a disquieting place for the visitor. It strikes a minatory note. . . ." Brooding mountains dominate the landscape, and even in the height of the summer with the promise of all the fun times ahead, there is a palpable ominousness. Osbert Lancaster (1947:197) wrote that

> Crete, to a greater extent, perhaps, than any other place in the world, certainly any place of similar size, possesses a power strangely to stir the imagination, even of those who have never been there. . . .

The deep-seatedness of this assonance is illustrated in three ways. First, sitting uneasily between Europe, Asia, and Africa, the island has been regularly invaded since its first settlement by Neolithic farmers about nine thousand years ago (Broodbank and Strasser 1991:237; Dickinson 1994:31). In the common era, Crete was successively occupied by Saracens, Venetians, and Ottomans. In the nineteenth century, its location gave it strategic importance in world geopolitics and for this reason the so-called Great Powers (Britain, France, and Russia) were unwilling to give it independence at the same time as it was given to the rest of the Greece. Its latest occupation occurred between 1941 and 1944 when German and Italian garrisons took control of the island. The horrors and deprivations of that period are still remembered vividly by those who experienced them. The island has been tossed around like a scrap of meat between competing powers for centuries. It continues still; today large segments of the northern coastline are taken over by the occupying hordes of tourists for the summer months. Consequently, although modern Cretans and indeed Greeks in general need the foreign currency that tourism brings, many are ambivalent toward tourism (to say the least). I was vividly reminded of how tourism changes people during our stay in Rethymno. Our stay covered the late winter period into May and the beginning of the tourist season. The town, especially along the waterfront east of the Old Town by the harbor, emerged like a butterfly from its chrysalis in a few short weeks. Slowly but quite perceptibly, the town geared itself to dealing with the influx of ephemeral visitors, to the point that the checkout attendants at the local supermarket, who had begun to treat us almost as members of the local community, treated us now like any other tourist, to be politely served and got out of the shop as quickly as possible. A wall was back between us.

Second, colonization for two hundred or so years by the Ottoman Empire (1669–1898) gave the island a profoundly conflicted existence as it was pulled between the East and the West.[4] The island was truly conflicted not just in the cultural but also in the spiritual sense (the depth to which the Ottoman presence is seared into the *spirit* of Crete

and its people is most famously documented in the novels of Nikos Kazantzakis). The Greek-speaking Muslim population was powerful both
politically and economically and in some locales, such as Rethymno,
constituted the majority of the population (Hamilakis 2006). Today, an
observant visitor to the island will experience virtually as much Ottoman culture as Western, whether in the architecture·of its harbor towns
or even in the particular styles of cooking. Although Cretans may acknowledge that it is all ancient history, it still is part of their national
psyche; the Ottoman occupation is not forgotten. One bureaucrat infa-
mously tried to destroy one of Rethymno's magnificent minarets during
the *junta* of 1967–1974 in order to Europeanize the past and to make the
island safe from possible future Turkish claims (Herzfeld 1991:57), an
act of cultural ethnic cleansing reminiscent of the removal of all non-
classical buildings from the Acropolis soon after Greek independence
(McNeal 1991) and the introduction in the nineteenth century of the ar-
tificial *katharevousa* in order to try to cleanse their language of barbaric
(i.e., Ottoman) elements (Morris 1994:23). Costis Davaras, ex-Ephor of
Antiquities for Eastern Crete and director of the Archaeological Museum
in Agios Nikolaos, who wrote the *Guide to Cretan Antiquities*, a book available at tourist shops on the island, described the Ottoman occupation of
the island as

> a sad time of exploitation, revolts and repressions, massacres
> and violent attempts at Islamization. Consequently the economy
> decayed, the population dropped by half, and *any form of higher
> civilization* ceased to exist. Crete, as well as the rest of Greece,
> almost lost its *European personality* [emphasis added].
>
> (Davaras 1976:xiv)

Third, this assonance characterized general attitudes toward the
Cretans themselves on the part of foreigners, including early archaeologists on the island. Robert Pashley explored Crete in 1834 and described
his journey in a now-classic early travelography, and he was clearly
smitten with the island and its culture. It cannot have been lost on
him that Cretan culture was profoundly infiltrated with a strong Ottoman element, yet for Pashley, the Turkish presence on the island was
a source only of cultural pollution, and he was unashamedly racist toward the Turks who lived on the island. For instance, he described his
guide thus: "My stupid Turk knew neither the road nor anything else"
(Pashley 1837:64–65), only acknowledging ten pages later on that his

guide "has only just come from Anatolia and knew no Greek. . . ." This assonance is visible, too, in how early archaeologists like Arthur Evans reveled in the island's Minoan past but showed diffidence toward its presence, and in how the modern tourist experience itself simultaneously embraces and shuns Cretan culture.

It was not until the early nineteenth century that Greece was considered safe enough for the intensive tourist experience that Italy had been able to offer during the heyday of the Grand Tour. Not only did Europeans begin coming to Greece, Americans too had begun arriving in numbers by the 1830s (Ware 2003:1755). However, the country soon caught up on what it had been missing, and by 1900 was a regular destination for wealthy Westerners (Morris 1994:18). Increasingly through the nineteenth century, Greece offered, as it had already done for the upper classes, the opportunity for middle and upper middle classes to gain *culture* (Ware 2003:1755), particularly by following prescribed itineraries of "'sacralized' sites in order to experience the sublime, the rhapsodic connection with the past" (Ware 2003:1756). The earliest recorded passages to Crete from the West were made early in the second millennium by pilgrims on their way to the Holy Land (Warren 2000:1), and the island generally suffered the same reputation as the mainland. In fact, Crete was even later in attracting foreign visitors in any numbers, for as recently as the last decade of the nineteenth century the island was wracked by popular uprisings against the Ottoman occupation. In the twentieth century, Crete, and its number one tourist attraction Knossos, finally became a stopover for Mediterranean cruise ships, but modern mass tourism was very late in coming to the island—made possible by the development of the airport at Iraklio in the 1960s, which allowed cheap air travel directly to the island (Pettifer 1994:75).

It takes only a cursory drive along the National Road, which hugs the northern coastline, to pick up a sense of why tourists come to Crete, or at least what they do when they get there. Its attractions are obvious: sun, sand, and, until recently, a relative inexpensiveness. East of Iraklio, towns like Mallia and Agios Nikolaos have largely been taken over by tourists during the peak summer seasons. The tone of these tourist traps is garish and loud, and they often become nationalist enclaves during the summer, sometimes with ugly consequences—for example, the beach fight between English and Dutch tourists a few years ago at Chersonnessos, a few miles west of Mallia (Pettifer 1994:76). The majority of visitors to Crete come as part of a package tour, in which a single payment to a tour company covers the costs of the airfare, hotel,

food, and some sightseeing trips. As is the case in many other Mediterranean resorts, local entrepreneurs and large hotel chains alike have
made a good profit in trying to make the traveler feel as little culture
shock as possible. Local inhabitants are ignored, except inasmuch as
they staff the necessary service industry or provide the virtually man-
datory Greek dances for evening dinner entertainments; this deliberate
distancing has been observed by others, in other parts of the world, for
example, Jamaica Kincaid (1989) in Antigua and Edward Bruner (2005)
in Kenya.

There are, of course, visitors to Crete who try to actively involve
themselves in the culture both present and past. They buy the guidebooks, they study the sites, and they take a respectful and appreciative
attitude to the island and its culture. And there is no implication here
that somehow this division, which I create mainly for didactic purposes,
has anything to do with socioeconomic classes. Anecdotally, I have
seen yobbish behavior by English tourists from both ends of the socioeconomic spectrum, at least as indicated by accent (a dangerous but
reasonably legitimate English conclusion on my part), as well as a serious appreciation of archaeological sites and the island's culture. Clearly,
these two extremes represent just that, ends of the spectrum.

The Theater of the Past

Knossos

The road to Knossos is signposted off the National Road. "Knossos
Antiquities," it says. Heading south, I pass drab, ugly shops and apart-
ments. A bend to the right, by the local hospital, and I glimpse the first
green of the countryside. Knossos is close, I know that, but I still can't
see it. Suddenly, as I pass what only the knowledgeable know are the
grounds of the Villa Ariadne, I see The Site. But not quite yet. What I
see first are the gimcrack tourist shops, the restaurants offering free
"Knossos Parking," and the row upon row of tour buses disgorging their
fares. Still no Knossos in sight as I buy my ticket, bypass the museum
shop, and head through the shaded, arbored walkway. But finally I spill
out with all the others onto the west courtyard of the site. There in all
his splendor is Arthur Evans, his bronze bust dominating the entrance
of the site and looking down on the visitors to his world. Disneyland
beckons, his past awaits. The rich are with you always.

Gournia

> Somewhere east of the tourist traps of the north coast is Gournia, a
> Bronze Age town, with well preserved streets and house foundations,
> all dominated by an "acropolis" vainly copying the sumptuous palaces
> to the west. Turning off the National Road, in relatively poor condition
> this far to the east of the island, I drive up a dirt track surrounded by
> olive groves. There was one attendant on duty who glumly gave me my
> ticket and brochure. No museum shop, virtually no site signs, just a
> Bronze Age town.

It is now necessary to focus on their experiences when tourists engage
with the Minoan past. I preface this discussion with Shanks's (1992:81)
observation that "in the archaeological theatre the discovered past is
the play and archaeologists the actors who work on the text producing
a performance, releasing some meanings of the past for an audience."
The poetics of the presented past shapes meaning and discourse (cf.
Shanks 1992; Tilley 1993).

Knossos and Gournia exemplify how the Minoan past is presented
to the public audience and how the past is indeed a performance. Both
of the sites are significant from a strictly academic point of view for
the different types of information they have provided archaeologists:
Knossos the grand palace, the capital, excavated by the dean of Minoan
archaeology, Arthur Evans; Gournia, a working town with at best a provincial *palace*, and excavated by a female, Harriet Boyd Hawes, in the
early part of the twentieth century when that gender was scarce on
the ground anywhere in archaeology. Yet how the sites are treated in
terms of public access (by which I mean not just physical but intellectual access) is rather different. As Chapter 2 has demonstrated, the state
of Minoan archaeology is in flux as old ideas are jettisoned and new
paradigms, assumptions, and interpretations come to the fore. And yet
very little of this controversy filters down to the tourist brochures, the
guidebooks, and so on.[5] Indeed, the public is presented with a Minoan
past that is in large measure simply out of date. For example, Gournia
is not just a *town*, yet that is how it is described in most guidebooks and
so the original portrayal of Gournia remains. Authentic and inauthentic
dissolve. Sites are not "truer" or "falser," or "still unclear"; they just are.

Although there is much overlap, I have for didactic purposes organized how the past is presented to the public into two different media:
the verbal and the visual, each of which has its own specific forms of
authority that persuade the tourist that its past is the only past, the accurate past, the true past. The verbal is communicated either through

written word, such as visitors' guides, or through spoken word, such as government-sanctioned guided tours of the sites. In both cases, their evocation of the past is powerful, with an apparent legitimacy and authenticity that is not to be questioned by the casual visitor. The visual is presented primarily through archaeological sites that have to varying degrees been reconstructed for public access and through museums that display a selection of material culture. These facilities are usually under the care and maintenance of state agencies. Separately these media are powerful, but together they provide a totality of verbal and visual imagery that is powerful and convincing (cf. Joyce 2002:2).

The repeated appearance of particular sites and museums and particular facts and points of emphasis in the print media exerts a powerful influence not just on what places tourists visit, but also on what they come to understand about the past. Information provided by the officially appointed guides at the sites and museums tends also to have the same aura of authority in terms of how they direct visitors to a particular past.

The power of narrative has been well ventilated in the literature. Howard-Malverde (1997:13) has noted how "narrative can create a sense of inevitability, a naturalising sense of the unquestionable in the given order of things." The "guidebook functions . . . like scriptures that reveal the already existent imperative truth of God's creation . . ." (Castañeda 1996:4). In general, travel writing is "a process of inscription and appropriation . . . [it] spins webs of colonizing power" (Duncan and Gregory 1999:3), which helped to establish Europe as metaphysically different from the rest of the world. Derek Gregory (1999:116) accurately describes this process as scripting, "a developing series of steps and signals, part structured and part improvised, that produces a narrativized sequence of interactions through which roles are made and remade by soliciting responses and responding to cues." Scripting converts "sites" into "sights" (Gregory 1999:145), and allows us to see "the ways in which travel writing is intimately involved in the 'staging' of particular places: in the simultaneous production of 'sites' that are linked in a space-time itinerary and 'sights' that are organized into a hierarchy of cultural significance" (Gregory 1999:116).

Verbal information is offered to the visitor to Crete in six ways: Web pages, guidebooks, pamphlets provided by the GNTO, on-site brochures, government-trained guides or docents, and local inhabitants. Web pages are a relatively new and sometimes unreliable way for the visitor to find out about an area's archaeology. They sometimes suffer from the universal problem of the Internet, which is that there is no control over the information put out; for instance, although most scholars still find the Phaistos disk undecipherable, the number of purported translations is quite remarkable (a simple Google search can demonstrate this quite easily). However, reputable web pages are in abundance, and these provide a reliable source of information on sites.

Guidebooks come in all shapes, sizes, and contents. Some cater to the visually inclined reader. The *Dorling Kindersley* series is an excellent example of this genre, and is characterized by multicolored drawings of how the sites may have looked. Others keep pictures to a minimum and concentrate on written descriptions. Freely (1988) is an outstanding example of a literate and informed description of the island and its sites, but there are many others of equal quality. The most scholarly of the guidebooks probably belong to the *Blue Guide Series*, with Crete having its own (Cameron 2003). It is characterized by a detailed conventional chronology of the Minoan period and comprehensive site descriptions and maps. It is written dispassionately, in keeping with its scholarly aura, an aura augmented by its lack of color pictures. Crete has not been immune to the increased popularity of travel writing over the past twenty-five years. Recent entries include Unsworth's (2004) *Crete* and MacLean's (2004) *Falling for Icarus*, both of which exemplify a common theme amongst such books of somewhat romanticizing the island and its inhabitants.

The pre-trip preparation and prospecting introduce the would-be visitor to the myth (Dufour 1978) and prepare him or her for the period of separation and liminality. The prospective tourist glances through the glossy brochures, calls up Internet Web pages, or delves into guidebooks in the local library. The visit to the foreign country is portrayed as exotic, as a paradise on Earth. So, at this stage, archaeological sites must play their parts and put on their best face. Superlatives abound: Knossos is "one of the most amazing archaeological sites" (*Fodor's Guide* 1999:394). The *Insight Guide* (p. 109) describes Knossos as "one of the archaeological wonders of the world. . . . The very name conjures up memories of the Labyrinth and the minotaur, King Minos, Daedalus and Icarus, Theseus and Ariadne, and all those other *fabled* [emphasis added] figures." The GNTO's brochure on Crete begins, "Crete, land of Daidalos and Ikaros. Of Minoan vases and famous frescoes." The Lonely Planet guide to the Greek Islands has a whole box devoted to the *Myth of the Minotaur*. The 2005 GNTO advertisements rely directly on the spinning of myth to entice the tourist. The banner headline *Live your Myth in Greece*; the young hard bodies overlooking an azure sea; and there in the corner is an Eros-like figure firing his arrow. And the text: *Greece: a land of mythical dimensions. Where the spirit of hospitality welcomes you as a modern god. And the siren song draws you into its deep blue waters. Where a gentle breeze through ancient ruins seems to whisper your name. And a dance until dawn can take on Dionysian proportions. In Greece, the myths are still very much alive. And in amongst them sits your own . . . patiently waiting for you to live it.* A Web page entitled *Greece Holiday and Travel Guide* (www.crete.uk.com) similarly encapsulates how the allure of the past is folded into the tourist experience:

> Whatever category you fall into—self-sufficient "Lonely Planet" backpacker or money-to burn "can't last a minute without my laptop" businessman—the highlight of your holiday will undoubtedly be a visit to the breathtaking Minoan Palace of Knossos. The secrets of the ancient but highly sophisticated Minoan civilisation lay hidden for nearly 3,000 years until a British archaeologist started excavating the palace site in the early 1900s.

> The treasures uncovered by his team together represent one of the most important archaeological discoveries the world has ever seen. Where else can you see Europe's oldest throne, still in its original place, and the en-suite bathroom of a Minoan queen who had the honour of gracing the world's first ever "flushing toilet"?

> The biggest sceptic and hardest heart couldn't fail to be moved by the site where myths, legends, recorded history and fairytales have merged into one giant Disney-style world of irresistible fact and fiction. Only on Crete is it possible to visit the reputed birthplace and hideout of Zeus, the king of the gods.

At this point, already the descriptions of the sites no longer just convey knowledge. They are overtures to the opera, preludes to the main act, with frothy melodies and felicitous phrasing. The would-be visitor has now been drawn into the magical world of the past. The spider's web is now all around him—he is pulled closer to the center of the web. And we must not be shy in seeing the archaeological site as an enticement to enter paradise. The tourist is deliberately enchanted, like a child entering a magic kingdom. But cleverly the myth is wrapped around a core of scientific fact, and this dissolves the distinction between the authentic and the inauthentic; the visitor is now prepared to believe everything that he or she is shown. Indeed, we might well agree with Russell's (2006:12) observation that conceptions of the past are acquired by many tourists through a variety of sources and "consumptive choices of where to go on holiday," and archaeology is used merely to support their conceptions. Can, then, even a scientifically constituted archaeology provide an antidote to what the tourists already think they know about the past?

Once in-country, the tourist is confronted by further sources of verbal information. Free tourist brochures found in hotel foyers, travel agency offices, and the like are powerful sources of information on the Minoan past. They all emphasize the largest sites and the most opulent treasures. The final source of verbal information comes from the official guides who are the only ones sanctioned by Greek law to lead groups around sites. The next chapter looks specifically at the training these guides undergo and why it is structured the way it is. At this point, it is sufficient to note that these guides are instructed to provide only uncontroversial information about the Minoan past, such as chronology, architectural details of the palaces, and aspects of social structure. My experience with different guides over the years is that all of them are extremely knowledgeable about the sites and museums and about Greek prehistory and history. However, it is clear that they are not employed to enter an open dialogue with their audience about the past. Rather, their presentations are linear and "factual." The result is that questions from the audience remain solidly within the parameters of the established discourse. I cannot remember anyone ever questioning the interpretation put forward by the guides or the context in which these interpretations were originally made. So, to repeat a point in Chapter 1, while tourists are not unthinking automata (cf. Bruner 2005:12), nevertheless their *agency* is reactive and bounded.

The visual is a strong medium of discourse, and visual consumption is an important topic in tourism studies (cf. Crawshaw and Urry 1997:194; Russell 2006). Rojek and Urry (1997:5) argue that sight has often been viewed as "the noblest of the senses," and given that the scientific method is based on observation, and that the West privileges sight over smell, taste, or touch (Hamilakis 2002d:122), we would expect that what is observed by the tourist is, therefore, a particularly strong medium of persuasion. The emphasis on the visual is the result of a variety of "social discourses organized by professionals, including photographers, travel writers, travel agents, tour operators, TV presenters and tourism policy makers" (Crawshaw and Urry 1997:176). Illustrations have historically been a key factor in how the past has been presented to the public (Moser 2001: 280), and it is likely that tourists simply get more of their information visually, from guidebooks or visiting the sites, than through actually reading literature: "visual impressions hold fast"

(Kristiansen 1992:12). "[M]aterial messages operate over longer time-spans than do verbal or active signals" (Fletcher 1989:37). In the West, physical (visual) meaning and transcendental meaning (a là Merriman 1996) have been conflated so that the latter cannot exist without the former.[6] However, because visual messages "blend scientific knowledge with accepted or assumed frames of reference" (Moser 2001:28), the power of these messages can easily be undervalued. Perhaps for this reason, discussion of the visual medium has too often in the past been seen as "unproblematic and relegated to the less prestigious arena of 'public archaeology'" (Moser 2001:263–264).

Archaeological Sites

Closeted in an air-conditioned coach, the tourist is parachuted into a locus removed from the real present and the real past (if such can indeed exist), persuaded to a willing suspension of disbelief made only easier by the apparent authority with which the past is presented. Like a pilgrim, the tourist is taken back to his or her essential roots, shown the secrets of the past, with no dissent possible. The tourist can ask questions, but only for enlightenment not for dialogue.

Publicly accessible archaeological sites are generally open to the public for some period of the day or season, and they offer a variety of amenities. The Appendix provides a description of each of the sites, including the type and quality of information available for the casual visitor. The ranking of these sites according to the information and amenities available can be examined in Table 4.1. At a minimum each provides with the admission price a small brochure that gives abbreviated site histories. At most they boast small museums and museum shops and are surrounded (as in the case of Knossos) by privately owned shops selling a variety of tourist wares. Kato Zakro is not in the same league as the other three palaces, having only the obligatory payment booth, a status probably reflective of its distance from Iraklio (approximately 75 miles).

In terms of their degree of restoration, the archaeological sites fall between the spectrum ends of attractions as defined by Cohen (1995:15): (1) natural, with no alteration to sites for tourists; (2) specifically created for tourist purposes, although none of them was specifically created just for tourism (notwithstanding Evans's problematic reconstruc-

Table 4.1 *Publicly Accessible Archaeological Sites and Their Amenities*

	Booth	**Brochure**	**Site Signs**	**Museum**	**Gift Shop**
Agia Triada	X	X	X	O	O
Amnisos	O	O	O	O	O
Armeni	X	O	O	O	O
Chamaizi	O	O	O	O	O
Chania	O	O	X	O	O
Gournia	X	X	X	O	O
Kato Zakro	X	X	X	O	O
Kommos	O	O	O	O	O
Knossos	X	X	X	X	X
Mallia	X	X	X	X	X
Nirou Khani	X	O	X	O	O
Palaikastro	X	O	X	O	O
Phaistos	X	X	O	X	X
Phourni	X	O	X	O	O
Sklavokambos	O	O	O	O	O
Tourkogeitonia	O	O	O	O	O
Tylissos	X	X	O	O	O
Vathypetro	X	O	X	O	O

Key: X = Present, O = Absent

tion of Knossos [Klynne 1998; Driessen 1999; Hitchcock 1999; Palyvou 2003]). The palaces are by far the most reconstructed of the public sites, Knossos being the most extreme (Figure 4.1). Evans's *reconstitutions,* to use his term (MacGillivray 2000:292), were mostly conducted between 1922 and 1930 (Papadopoulos 2005:110) and themselves are now undergoing archaeological restoration. Opinions are divided. On the one hand, MacGillivray (2000:293–294) retells some of the more trenchant criticisms of the Knossos Restoration; Collingwood, the Oxford historian, compares it to "garages and public lavatories"; the Canadian Prime minister, Pierre Trudeau "marveled at how the Minoan architect had predicted the shapes and colors of Art Deco . . . and asked '*When* did you say this place was restored?'" Evelyn Waugh, never one to miss the chance for an epigram, commented that the site's "painters have tempered their zeal for reconstruction with a predilection for covers of 'Vogue'" (Lapatin 2002:120) and referred to the site as "a place of oppressive wickedness" (MacGillivray 2000:293). On the other hand, some

Figure 4.1 *Palace Room, Knossos*

have welcomed the restoration. Henry Miller, a man whose snobbishness (sometimes straight ahead and sometimes in reverse, but always there) was exceeded only by his prolixity, wrote

> However Knossus [sic] may have looked in the past, however it may look in the future, this one which Evans has created is the only one I shall ever know. I am grateful to him for what he did, grateful that he had made it possible for me to descend the grand staircase, to sit on that marvelous throne chair the replica of which at the Hague Peace Tribunal is now almost as much of a relic of the past as the original.
>
> (Miller 1941:121)

The majority of visitors to Knossos do respond positively to the reconstruction (Papadopoulos 2005:118), and my experience with students and visitors to Knossos and Phaistos is that they prefer Knossos, if only because it gives them a better feel for what a Minoan palace would (or may) have looked like (cf. Lowenthal 1985:282).[7] Nor should we be overly superior about the accuracy of Evans's reconstruction. Papado-poulos (2005:110) has pertinently asked what would have happened to the site if Evans had not acted, pointing out that more recent investiga-tions at the site and at other sites throughout the Mediterranean have resulted in excavations that have not been followed up with adequate conservation procedures.

At the other end of the spectrum are most of the other sites. They have been stabilized so that the effects of natural erosion and weathering are slowed down, and in some cases particularly fragile areas are roofed over (e.g., Mallia, Kato Zakro, Palaikastro, Nirou Khani.) The site shelter at Mallia cost over $500,000 (Stanley-Price 2003:276). In most sites, the walls and other standing structures have not been built up, so the visitor is mostly walking around a site that is smaller in height than the original.

The treatment of Knossos stands far above every other site on the is-land in terms of visitor access and facilities. However, not even all of the individual sites that properly form part of the overall Knossos complex are accessible to the public; only the palace is open. And, as is shown by the accompanying box, which contains my diary notes from site visits in 2002, sites other than the big three of Knossos, Phaistos, and Mallia are given minimal advertisement or public access. I would sug-gest that the lack of funds is only partially to blame for this access. For even if Knossos does require a great deal of upkeep and given that its restoration is problematical, could not these other sites be developed? Of course, the answer is no, because only Knossos preserves the myth, and it is the myth that sells.

Given the way tourists present themselves to sites and sites are presented to them, there is no real opportunity for discourse with the medium itself. Rather, the tourist is only passively stimulated by the site experience. There is, to use Böröcz's (1996:11) phrase, an "inherent voyeurism of the tourist experience," and this is certainly the case with archaeological sites. Urry's (1990) book *The Tourist Gaze* shows how the gaze "locks the imagery into the 'depth-less' dimension of visuality." Thus, archaeological sites—as monuments of a past—lose their diachronic dy-namism; they are recreated as a timeless and depthless entity.

The visitor to a Minoan site is treated almost as a child (cf. Dann 1996). If one is lucky, signposts or guidebooks lead the visitor through a pre-set procession, even if the particular path is not what an ancient visitor to the site would have experienced. The consequent loss of ex-perience for a modern visitor is well exposed by an insightful paper by Lansing Fair (2004) who suggests that the modern visitor should enter Knossos as an ancient visitor would have done. As Palyvou (2003:230) has also noted, tourists are restricted to paths that do not reflect the circulatory pattern of the movement in Minoan architecture. If site managers really want to cement the mythical dream world of Knossos, this would be a good way. It has been argued (Duke 2006) that the visit to a tightly controlled site like Knossos is akin to a ritual visit (full of etiquette and expected behavior) to a site of memorialization (the origins of Western civilization) that metaphorically evokes a message about the past and the present (the primacy of social inequality). A metaphor, which I argue is what Knossos is, is especially powerful at evoking messages because it seems so natural (Lakoff 1996).

As the island's premier site, Knossos dominates public perceptions of Cretan archaeology, as historically it and its excavator Evans dominated the discipline. The site receives more care and attention from the Archaeological Service than any other site on the island , and this plus its reconstruction means that it is more visually stunning than other sites, like Phaistos or Mallia, thus becoming more imprinted on the memory and more important in the past, too. Sometime after my visit to Knossos in 2003, the old signs had been replaced with more informative plaques, probably in preparation for the 2004 Olympic Games and the expected increase in visitors to the site. The information is still basic, in that it focuses on the functions of individual features and the more noticeable artifacts found in them. However, most significantly there were some new signs that admitted to the heavy interpretation and reconstruction that Evans had imposed. For example, the sign describing the so-called *piano nobile* announced: "the grand staircase and the upper floor to which it leads are largely Evans' creation. Evans thought that it had a function rather like the first floor of Italian Palazzi of the Renaissance." However, at other sites the signage is still sparse, even at Phaistos where there were very few signs indicating what room or complex one was actually in. Sparseness of information is even more pronounced at the smaller sites. One exception is Palaikastro, which, although located on the east end of the island, has detailed plaques documenting the construction history of the site, courtesy of its excavators from the British School.

Museums

If representations such as Knossos stimulate *magic* thought, whereby meaning is assigned by the totality of associations, then museums and their collections stimulate *scientific* thought and objective knowledge (cf.

MacCannell 1976:78–80; Graburn 1977:19). The ordered rows of display cases, each with their little cardboard or plastic signs, are there to educate, to impose an external meaning to the past. The arrangement of materials in museums is an especially powerful medium of communication. For "in looking at a museum display, it is not the subject of the display that requires understanding, but how the arrangement of material culture produces particular meanings about that subject" (Moser 2001:269). It is little wonder that in the nineteenth century, public mus-eums were given such a profoundly serious role, namely the legitimization of heritage and the nation-state (Stone and Molyneux 1994; Arnold and S. Ditchfield 1998; MacDonald 1998). They serve as time machines to take us to one particular past, and in so doing invite such questions as (1) Who is empowered by certain modes of display? (2) What state or economic interests impinge? (3) To what extent do visitors define museums on their own terms? (4) How do forms and techniques enable particular readings? (MacDonald 1998:4).

The museums on Crete range in size downward from the large facility at Iraklio, which, despite the very heavy number of visitors, sometimes in groups of thirty or more, still manages to allow reasonably good visual access to the materials on display. The smaller museums at Chania, Rethymno, Agios Nikolaos, and Siteia are far less crowded, and consequently offer a more tasteful atmosphere. There is also a small site museum at Mallia, which displays some of the objects recovered from excavations.[8] These facilities fulfill the role of educating the public about a Minoan past, but it would not be overly disparaging to describe Cretan museums as traditional. The Iraklio museum is a striking example of this trait. It is housed in what the Berlitz guidebook (1996: 190) accurately describes as "an uninspired concrete blockhouse." The collections are organized chronologically to a spatial plan originally laid down between 1951 and 1964 by Platon and Alexiou (cf. Platon's [1962] guide to the museum). Each gallery is assigned a particular period of time, and the visitor simply has to walk anti-clockwise on the ground floor to cover the first thirteen of the twenty galleries. Row upon row of treasures confirm the magnificence of Cretan material culture. The display cases each have informational plaques, but these are minimal, offering if appropriate the name of the object and always its date and provenance.

In the summer the Iraklio museum experience is daunting. During one visit in May 2004 I sat for about thirty minutes in the upstairs gallery of the museum, where the gold *Ring of Minos* and other treasures are displayed. The average number of visitors in the gallery at any one time was about twenty people. So, at all times the ring was very accessible for inspection. The average stay was about eight seconds (one group was exceptional in taking a whole minute). The visitors flitted from case to case. Many appeared to know they needed to look at this material, but I wonder if they knew why. Frankly, the attitude I sensed amongst the visitors was jadedness—"not another priceless treasure," I could almost hear them saying. Like many visitors, I suspect, I always feel tired and irritated at myself. I know I am looking at magnificent pieces, but fighting my way through the "hordes" always leaves me mentally and physically exhausted.

The situation is somewhat different at the smaller provincial museums at Chania, Rethymno, Archanes, Agios Nikolaos, and Siteia. They are funded from the overall provincial archaeological budgets and so must compete with mandated emergency rescue projects. They must also strike a balance between the security needs of their most important pieces (which often end up being housed elsewhere) and retaining local possession of them. Consequently, these museums offer a slightly different version of the past. Objects are still traditionally (i.e., chronologically) displayed but because most of the major finds (i.e., the treasures) are in Iraklio, these museums display materials that are more mundane and more reflective of everyday activities (these small regional museums still do have some treasures on display; for example, the collection of Linear A tablets at Siteia).

The museums at Chania and Rethymno are located in converted historic buildings, and this itself lends a charm to the museum experience that is quite lacking at Iraklio. The Chania museum is located in the church of the old Venetian monastery of St. Francis. It concentrates on local finds and sites. There is a very good map of the sites to be found in Chania province, and then the visitor is left to wander through the different periods. The whole museum is in essentially one large room and so you are not *guided* in any particular direction. The descriptive notes within each cabinet of finds were impressive in that although they were brief, they offered more than the "bare facts." What stood out was the regular reference to male vs. female in the tomb offerings.

As at Chania, the public part of the Rethymno Museum is one room (much smaller than Chania's), the whole museum complex being part of the Venetian fortezza that dominates the town (for many years the museum was housed in the old Venetian loggia in the center of the old town). The first display is a map of the different types of sites in the Rethymno area. One then proceeds to wall cases that take one through the various periods of occupation, from Neolithic to Roman. Most of the artifacts are pottery, but there are bone tools on display and some high-quality larnakes. The Agios Nikolaos museum was built in the 1960s and like the other provincial museums concentrates on the finds from nearby sites. The Siteia Museum is the most recent, opening in 1984. The items on display are organized chronologically. The Archanes museum is housed in a single room in a converted building. As in the other museums, the cases are tasteful and informative, concentrating on the more mundane items of material culture. This museum also displayed a reconstruction, complete with skeleton, of a burial from a nearby site. Although these smaller museums are organized in a traditional chronological manner, nevertheless their concentration on local sites and finds provides a perspective on provincial Minoan life that is largely missing at the Iraklio museum. But how many casual visitors end up in these provincial museums? When we visited the museum at Agios Nikolaos, the town was throbbing with tourists, yet we were the only two in the place.

Other Visual Sources of Information

Other sources of visual information are found on the admission tickets and in the on-site brochures that are provided for each visitor as part of the entrance fee. The fronts of most comprise a picture of a rare or spectacular artifact. The GNTO provides glossy tourist brochures; the one for Crete has on its first page a copy of the dolphin fresco from Knossos followed by two pages of beach scenes. The juxtaposition is jarring. If the Minoan sites are indeed world-famous, surely they deserve higher status than just another entertainment spot. What must tourists think of them? That they really are important as the origins of Western civilization? Or are they just another nice place to visit?

Such, then, are the various sources of information that the tourist receives about the past. What type of information is provided, however? As important, what is left out? Combining all these sources of information offers us a good idea of what type of past is presented to the public, what is voiced and what is silenced.

The Minoan past is presented as the first and, directly or by implication, the ancestor to all later Western civilization. So, the *Insight Guide* (p. 21) describes the Minoan culture as Europe's "first sophisticated civilization." *Fodor's* (1999:384) is even more evocative: "Around 1500 B.C. while the rest of Europe was still in the grip of primitive barbarity, one of the most brilliant and amazing civilizations the world was ever to know approached its final climax." The Web page *Greece Holiday and Travel Guide* (www.crete.uk.com) asks "Where else can you see Europe's oldest throne?" "The Greek islands were the homes of two of Europe's earliest civilizations, the Cycladic and the Minoan" (*Lonely Planet* 2000b:17). The purported primacy of Minoan civilization turns up in all sorts of unexpected places. For example, the informational video shown to visitors to the Peza Wine Cooperative begins with "Knossos, the birthplace of European civilization."

All the site brochures provided with the admission ticket, regardless of the site type, offer the same type of information. The brochures typically comprise a colored site map that provides a chronological history of the site itself and a typology of the site's individual features. The accompanying text is always minimal, describing the site's individual features and its culture history and perhaps making a brief reference to where its artifacts are now housed. A further point is that the sources of information on the Minoan past tend to concentrate on the climax of Minoan architecture and material culture. Guidebooks are invariably organized around a chronology (the most detailed is in the *Blue Guide to Crete*) that charts the increasing complexity and sophistication of Minoan prehistory and the progression to a *higher* form of society. The *Insight Guide* (p. 22) expounds that "around 2000 B.C., Cretan society took another major step forward." Site brochures typologize the historical sequences of architectural development at the sites. The Knossos brochure (Figure 4.2), like all the others, has an excellently detailed map of the site that shows its chronological development. The opening paragraph starts with "its superb architectural composition, its functionality, and its flawless construction is considered to be a typical example of the Minoan palaces." So, brilliance was apparently just the norm for ancient Minoans. Such chronologies emphasize that the past is about change and more explicitly change toward greater social and cultural complexity. This directly mirrors one of the most important paradigms in Aegean archaeology, namely the neo-evolutionary model espoused by Renfrew (1972), an influential and in some circles almost revered Aegean archaeologist (Kotsakis 1991:81). I will revisit this model and its attendant critique in the following chapter. For now it is sufficient to point out that such evolutionary models naturalize the notion of greater social complexity, with the attendant implication that social ranking—class—is also an expected and natural social condition that can be fine for all concerned.

Visual emphasis is placed on sites and objects associated with the elite of Minoan society. The phrase "the glories of the Minoan past,"

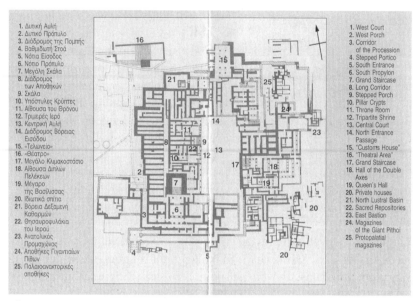

Figure 4.2 *Page from Knossos site brochure*

from the *Lonely Planet Greek Islands* (2000b:253), is typical of how the past is described. The guidebooks have pictures of the reconstructions of Knossos, the Phaistos disk, the frescoes, the snake goddesses, or the equisite rhyta. The site brochures continue this emphasis. Knossos's features the *La Parisienne* fresco, Phaistos's the disk, Mallia's the bee pendant, Agia Triada's the Harvester's Vase, and Kato Zakro's the restored rock crystal rhyton (Gournia's is different, with a view of the streets of the town). One of the GNTO's free glossy tourist brochures for Crete has on its first page a copy of the dolphin fresco from Knossos. Then there are two pages of beach scenes followed by a one-page spread that contains a large picture of the north portico at Knossos and three much smaller pictures of pithoi from Phaistos, a rock crystal rhyton from Kato Zakro, and the site of Tylissos. Another glossy brochure put out by the GNTO has archaeological sites in the list of things-to-do. The brochure's visual presentation emphasizes Knossos, with the sites worth visiting listed alphabetically in a small-print, single-space glossary at the end of the brochure. A pamphlet sponsored by Telestet, a leading Greek cellular phone company, entitled *Crete, the most important archaeological sites,* lists only Knossos, Phaistos, and Gortyna. Its front page is taken up by the Phaistos disk, a snake goddess figurine, and the throne room at Knossos (Figure 4.3). A pamphlet put out by the Tourline Company has just one figure, the reconstructed priest-king fresco from Knossos.

The palaces (especially Knossos) draw the most tourists, precisely because they are directed to them. Table 4.2 lists the frequency in the eleven tourist books of the eighteen sites and the six museums that were visited. Only the four palaces and Gournia have a 100 percent rating. Although Gournia gets a high rating, nevertheless the site has far fewer visitor facilities than Knossos, Mallia, and Phaistos. It can be suggested, therefore, that the artifacts and the sites of the elite of society are those that figure most prominently in the brochures and the museums and they are the ones that get the most attention. This emphasis comes at the expense of a greater understanding of and appreciation of the lifeways of the nonelite.

However, we must not worry too much about the nonelite, for this highly structured society was a paradise for all. Everybody pros-

Figure 4.3 *Brochure front page*

pered under the benevolence of the island's rulers. Some guidebooks such as the *Insight Guide* (p. 23) describe the Minoans as having "a monarchical central power in Knossos." It stresses that this "island kingdom" lived under a *Pax Minoica* (p. 24), and that "all the arts reflected the people's peaceful way of life." Only on p. 28 does it acknowledge the existence of the poor: "Houses from the area around Siva were poor, without kitchen, lavatory or even a stable." But life was still good: "Minoan frescoes show women participating in games, hunting, and religious festivals on apparently equal terms with men" (p. 31). *Discover Greece* (1996:195) pursues the same theme of paradise on earth: ". . . around 1400 BC, life at the Palace was comfortable. Energy was devoted to sport, not warfare, and the good things of life—especially food and wine—were plentiful." The *Lonely Planet Greek Islands* guide describes "a society that was powerful, wealthy, joyful and optimistic"; "women enjoyed a respected position in

Table 4.2 *Popularity of Citation in Selected Guide Books (N = 11)*

Archaeological sites	Frequency
Agia Triada	11
Amnisos	2
Armeni	3
Chamaizi	2
Chania	8
Gournia	11
Kato Zakro	11
Knossos	11
Kommos	3
Mallia	11
Nirou Khani	2
Palaikastro	4
Phaistos	11
Phourni	2
Sklavokambos	2
Tourkogeitonia	8
Tylissos	9
Vathypetro	5

Museums	Frequency
Agios Nikolaos	7
Archanes	1
Chania	9
Iraklio	11
Rethymno	9
Siteia	7

society . . . [however] . . . There is evidence of human sacrifice practiced at least on one occasion, although probably in response to an extreme external threat" (2000b:254). So they were forced to practice human sacrifice rather than doing it voluntarily. I was glad to read that as it would have spoiled my opinion of them otherwise.

It is now time to initiate the discussion on why this picture of the Minoan past is the one that is presented to the public. The intensity of study in Minoan archaeology has sometimes not been matched by the broadness of research scope (rather like the American Southwest, which occupies a somewhat analogous position in the development of American archaeology). Hamilakis (2002a:4) offers a list of issues that Minoan archaeologists still know little about: "social organization; links between economic and social practices, gender relationships, power dynamics, and the routines of everyday life." So perhaps it might be unfair to criticize their absence in public discourses on Minoan culture. Yet their absence in this discourse cannot be wholly excused, for it points to a fundamental issue of public archaeology; that is, the degree to which the public is allowed into the academic debate on interpreting the past and determining what should be studied. There is a wall between the past and the public, and the latter is only allowed controlled glimpses of that past. The public, despite being the source of revenue and in some cases the taxation that provides for site stabilization and site study, is cut out of any debate of what parts of the past to study and what is said about the past. The public passively receives what is offered. Contemporary archaeology, far from consolidating the positivist tradition that it adopted in the 1960s, is increasingly recognizing that explanatory paradigms change in the light of contemporary political conditions; an archaeological site is best seen not as the end of a story from the past but the beginning of a debate about the present (Duke 1993). Yet no attempt is made to draw the public into any consideration of alternative arrangements of the Cretan past. As elsewhere in the world, the public is treated as unsophisticated and incapable of understanding the nuances of the discipline. Additionally, it is remarkable that despite the prevalence of female goddess figurines in the popular literature and the iconography that is used to sell the Minoan past, there is little consideration of the role of women in Minoan society. Some of the guidebooks narrate that women had an equal role in society and that Minoan religion had a large female component. However, there is little attempt to explore the nuances of what this might actually mean for the average Minoan female. Thirdly, in concentrating on the elite of Minoan society, the lower class becomes invisible. References to the poor of Minoan society are few. Finally, the lurid side of Minoan life gets little press in the public literature. The tourist is not made aware of the squalor and disease that undoubtedly was a part of Minoan life. In Chapter 3 I described a number of instances of possible human sacrifice and/or cannibalism. And yet with few exceptions (the *Insight Guide*, for example), little is made of this. Yet surely this would interest the public without embarrassing modern Cretans?

The choice of this past is the result of factors, both past and present and conscious and unconscious. Therefore, it is now incumbent on me to unpack these factors and show how they have contributed to what is offered to the public at archaeological sites on Crete. This is the focus of the next chapter.

Selected Diary Notes

3/13/2002, Chania: The site is not well signposted. There is an information plaque that shows the layout of the site, its main chronology, and the history of excavations.

3/19/2002, Agia Triada: There are no information plaques on the site and no path takes you around it and through it. There is nothing to stop you walking on the walls—in fact, it is almost impossible not to if you want to cover the whole site. The man at the booth apparently knew nothing about archaeology. A minor disappointment was the tombs to the north of the site, which had been described in every guidebook, were locked up, and he did not have the key.

3/30/2002, Sklavokambos: Easy to find as it is on the main highway, but the signpost is small. The site is fenced and closed and no information is available on site. It is even more difficult to visit because the site has no place in which to park and there is virtually no hard shoulder to the road. So it is dangerous to view.

4/2/2002, Tylissos: Well signposted. The site has no parking facilities but a local house offers free parking and the temptation of buying their lace and linen. Two custodians who spoke nothing but Greek. A rudimentary brochure given to us by the old lace lady—just giving the bare facts of the site. Not one signpost on the site itself and certainly nothing to differentiate the three different villas that make up the site. The site is overgrown with weeds— rather sad and shabby.

4/2/2002, Amnisos: It is very shabbily situated and looked after. Both of the complexes at the base of the hill are fenced off. The hilltop complex is overgrown and unmarked. The whole site is surrounded by detritus and garbage—an abandoned caravan.

4/3/2002, Phourni: Difficult to find all the different structures because there is no site map. The guard man very silent at first but I persevered and got some good information from him.

4/10/2002, Chamaizi: A single sign off the main road and then a very poor cart track took us to the site. It is spectacular but there is absolutely no information on this site at all.

4/26/2002, Palaikastro: Surprisingly well signposted and by far the best site signage. Clear maps of the different site areas.

NOTES

1. New prayer recommended in the 1970s by the Greek Orthodox Church, cited in Crick (1989:334).

2. Peckham (1999) has exposed this in a cleverly titled article, *The Exoticism of the Familiar and the Familiarity of the Exotic: Fin-de-siècle Travellers to Greece.*

3. I have used this literary term, which refers to an unexpected rhyme, a dissonance of words, as an appropriate metaphor for describing these conflicting emotions.

4. I have deliberately isolated Ottoman colonization because of its importance in understanding the course of Cretan history and for that matter the course of how early archaeological explorations on the island were conducted.

5. The data used in this chapter come from a variety of sources. First, I consulted all the guidebooks on Greece that were available at local bookstores and the local library in Durango, Colorado (something a prospective tourist would do): Baedeker's Mediterranean Islands (1984); *Berlitz Discover Greece* (1996); *Berlitz Travellers Guide to Greece* (1992); *Blue Guides. Greece* (Rossiter 1980); Dorling Kindersley, *Greek Islands* (1997); *Fodor's Guide* (1999); Insight Guide to Crete (n.d.); *Lonely Planet. Greece* (2000a); *Lonely Planet. Greek Islands* (2000b); *Michelin Tourist Guide to Greece* (1998); *Rough Guide to Greece* (1998). This step provided some baseline for what was described of the Minoan past for the public. Consulting these books also provided a list of sites and museums on the island, and their popularity was gauged by the number of times they were mentioned. A Google search in July of 2005 provided the following hits for each of the following sites: Knossos—27,400; Phaistos—6,730; Gournia—917; Kato Zakro—121; Mallia—663; Agia Triada—945; Vathypetro—243. Fieldwork consisted of visiting the most popular sites and museums, a total of eighteen sites and six museums, during the spring of 2002. The following sites were visited: Agia Triada, Amnisos, Armeni, Chamaizi, Chania, Gournia, Kato Zakro, Knossos, Kommos, Mallia, Nirou Khani, Palaikastro, Phaistos, Phourni, Sklavokambos, Tourkogeitonia, Tylissos, Vathypetro. The following museums were visited: Agios Nikolaos, Archanes, Chania, Iraklio, Rethymno, Siteia. The Appendix describes each of these.

6. This is not the case in many non-Western cultures. American Indians recognize traditional cultural properties as physically unaltered landscapes, for example, and in China ancient buildings can be added to or transformed into something virtually new without any loss of its spirit or meaning (Byrne 1991:275).

7. Some visitors are overwhelmed by the site. Last summer I was joined by a visitor on the west edge of the central courtyard at Knossos. He took one look, declared "wow, big place" and scanning his guidebook scurried on to the next point of importance.

8. Silverman (2006) has given site museums special consideration in a recent edited volume because they have the potential to change their presentations in light of new museological imperatives, and thereby to present a more dynamic and contemporary picture of the site and to engage the local community in a more active role.

CHAPTER FIVE

Constructing a Prehistory

It has been argued thus far that tourists are presented with a selective past at archaeological sites and museums, with certain aspects being emphasized and others silenced. This selectivity is the result of pouring the material remains of the past through two filters. The first filter is constructed of the academic interests and ideologies of professional archaeologists who have taken it upon themselves to recreate an objective and authoritative past. The second filter is constructed of the government bureaucrats, site managers, tourist entrepreneurs, and guidebook writers who put the past on display. The decisions leading to the creation of these filters can be understood only within their historical and contemporary contexts. In this chapter I identify five factors—hegemonies—that together have created the past that is on show to the public: colonialism and the rise of modernity; academic elitism; archaeological paradigms; state politics; economics. I will conclude this chapter by arguing that these hegemonies have been and still are so strong as to militate against meaningful local control of the Minoan past.

Although the concept of heritage has run through this book, both explicitly and implicitly, it is time to broach this subject in more detail, if only because tourist access to the Minoan past must be contextualized within the larger heritage industry. The Minoan past was appropriated early on as the origins of the overall Western heritage, and this role has infiltrated into the state ownership and control of the past, and its importance in providing a marketing tool to attract tourists. Heritage became an important bulwark in the promotion of the modern nation-state and nationalism,[1] whereby individual citizens were given a state—as well as a local—identity (Anderson 1983) and played an important role in the modernist project that both legitimized nineteenth century progress and at the same time offered refuge from it (Lowenthal 1985:102). It can be viewed either as an honest and unconsidered recognition of one's cultural roots or as an exploitative construction that invents spurious traditions for any number of purposes, such as nationalism, imperialism, or capitalist gain (cf. Hobsbawm and Ranger 1983),[2] or even as "a symptom of [a] country's industrial and social decline" as a community looks to the past to try to recover and relive old glories (Merriman 1996:377). Regardless of the motives behind it, pejorative or not, heritage as represented by "tokens of antiquity" is a concept "all but universally adopted" (Lowenthal 1994:302). For Merriman (1996:381–382), heritage has both an empirical (i.e., physical and material) and a transcendental (i.e., memory, attitudes, imagination) meaning. He distinguishes between the processes of heritage (e.g., physical preservation, the collecting of antiques) and the products of heritage (e.g., theme parks) as though the two were intellectually and ontologically independent entities. This is a template for how the past has been used traditionally by government entities, which is reflective of the traditional view of the archaeological record.

It is difficult to support the claims made by some (e.g., Urry 1990) that the promotion of a common heritage, be it national or Western, provides a democratized history. I would argue that even though the heritage industry has made the past (both general and specific) more accessible to previously uninterested groups, it has not allowed those groups to become actively involved in either its creation or interpretation. I say this for two reasons. First, one of the abiding issues with the creation of a particular heritage is that of identity: whose past is being presented? As cultural heritage is "packaged" for tourist consumption or nationalistic propaganda (Howell 1994:151), or for any other potential reason, it is surely clear that only certain classes of society are being catered to. It has been pointed out by Bennett (1988:64) that nineteenth century museums, while they may have been for the people, were not of the people; their purpose was to "map out geographies of taste and values" (Lumley 1988:2). Relatively little has changed in the intervening hundred years. There has, for example, been little change in the composition of visitors to museums over the past thirty years (Richards 1994:370–371), the appearance of a well-financed heritage industry not withstanding. Frequent museum visitors tend to be well-educated professionals (although there is some evidence that the audience is broadening). According to an early survey by Merriman (1989:15) for museum visitors of "high status," topics such as world history, state history, and national identity ranked most highly, with family history of least importance; those of "low status" ranked these issues in complete reverse order. Collins's (2004) analysis of the white working class of Southwark in southeast London argues that their culture is most deeply rooted in a landscape of home. Such conclusions are consonant with those of Gans (1962) and Campbell (1988) that working-class families tend to seek out the familiar. Similarly, Bodnar (1992) has differentiated between *official* and *vernacular* histories. This recognition has been late in coming to heritage and museum studies, it having been commonly assumed that *all* members of a society recognized and embraced only one particular heritage, a fallacy engendered in the nineteenth century and perpetuated still today. Even though democratization has expanded the definition of what the public is, museums still tend to authenticate official values directly and indirectly by subordinating or rejecting alternatives (Ames 1992:22, 24). Benavides (2004:6) has exposed Ecuadorian "historical memory as closely aligned to the hegemonic structure that both supports and reinforces a national identity and the nation-state's contemporary status quo—that is highly unequal class, racial, and gendered/sexual social structures."

The meaning of heritage for members of a particular community, however, can change; Hoyau (1988) gives a good example from contemporary France of this metamorphosis. And this possibility of change provides the potential that at different times different hegemonies will be served by the past. This potential does not preclude that older hegemonies will linger on in how the site is used. Quite the contrary, they linger on like an appendix awaiting its appendectomy, and the result is that the site or museum is a palimpsest not just of different stratigraphic levels and different artifact cases, but potentially a palimpsest of different ideologies and hegemonies, too. Sites on Crete and public access to them have been created by the five hegemonies to which I earlier alluded, and the following sections consider these individually.

Colonialism and the Rise of Modernity

> Every archaeological event . . . increased the prestige of Greece, but this prestige was translated into another symbol of Greece as a passive representation of the birth of the west.
>
> (Morris 1994:33)

I have combined colonialism and modernity into a single section because they together provide the essential context to understanding the birth of Minoan archaeology at the end of the nineteenth century. After the Ottoman occupation, Crete was temporarily controlled by the so-called Great Powers, albeit not to the extent or duration they imposed upon other colonies in their empires. While specific definitions of colonialism are problematical and beyond the scope of this current work (cf. Thomas 1994 and Gosden 2004 for stimulating discussions), of rather more utility for our purposes is to recognize the effects of colonial culture and the resultant intellectual imperialism, which subjugated not only contemporary Crete to the geopolitical needs of the Great Powers but also its past (and its present, too) to the intellectual needs of the West. Together they were instrumental in turning Crete and its archaeology into a fiefdom of foreign scholars—so that Crete was simultaneously colonized both militarily (albeit only temporarily) and archaeologically—and in establishing the academic elitism that pervaded Minoan archaeology.

Crete was little more than a pawn in western European geopolitics at the turn of the twentieth century and did not even gain complete independence until seventy-odd years after mainland Greece. The nineteenth century saw increasing unrest on Crete against prolonged Ottoman domination and in 1896, precisely the time when Evans was looking to excavate Knossos, the islanders revolted, not for the first time.[3] Ultimately, in order to preserve a peace during the transition to independence, the so-called Great Powers established garrisons on the island: the Russians at Rethymno, the British at Iraklio, the Italians in Hierapetra, and the French in Siteia and Spinalonga (McEnroe 2002:61). The island's sites were divided up for excavation and research, with most early archaeology being conducted by the British, French, and Italians (Hamilakis 2002a:3). The Haweses (1911:12) identified the British, Italians, and Americans as the three nations who "have worked in friendly rivalry to learn the buried history of Crete."[4]

The first generation of Minoan archaeologists lived during the birth of what Said (1978) has termed orientalism, an aesthetic that still dominates many arenas of political discourse, and which also profoundly influenced how those archaeologists interpreted the Minoan past. Orientalists "feared not . . . the destruction of Western civilization, but rather the destruction of the barriers that kept East and West from each other" (Said 1978:263). It was necessary at that time to make clear that Greece was not part of the Islamic east, the anti-Islamic element being almost as strong as philhellenism (McEnroe 2002:63).[5] Evans, the American Richard Seager, and others made the Minoans not just modern, but also as advanced as the Oriental civilizations (Lapatin 2002:55). It seems that at that time the ancient Orient was good only for providing ideas that the Greeks could then make their own (Morris 1994:21), and it was of fundamental importance to give European civilization a unique character (Kristiansen 1992:15). Therefore, it is not just coincidence that archaeology in the Mediterranean flourished at the same time as the collapse of the Ottoman Empire (McConnell 1989:107). With Evans at their helm the first Minoanists proclaimed Minoan civilization as ancestral to all subsequent European civilizations, one on par with Egypt and Mesopotamia, but, importantly, quite separate from them (Lapatin 2002:9–10; Padopoulos 2005:88). Just as ancient Greece was proclaimed in the nineteenth century to be "the idealized spiritual and intellectual ancestor of Europe" (Herzfeld 1989:1), so did the interpretation of Bronze Age Crete—as the putative ancestor of ancient Greece—become as important. David Hogarth in 1899 posed the question "whence originated this great early civilization of the Greek lands? And what in the end became of it? These are the questions that concern the world at large; for they bear in general on the mysterious origins of our civilization in Europe . . ." (Cullen 2001:7). Evans (1921:24) maintained that Crete was "the cradle of European civilization" until the day he died. An early synthesis of Cretan archaeology by the Haweses (1911:2) put Crete's primacy very baldly: "the Golden Age of Crete was the forerunner of the Golden Age of Greece, and hence all our western culture" (Hawes and Hawes 1911:2).

The conduct of archaeology during this period—and Evans truly was a product of the nineteenth century—must also be placed into the context of modernity (cf. Thomas 1994) and its intellectual support for the nation-state, *laissez-faire* capitalism, and the increasing reliance on science and technology as solutions to contemporary social problems. Modernity, however, came at a cost: (1) the experience of one's personal life as "a maelstrom" (Berman 1982:345), and (2) the need to make an individual accommodation to this maelstrom by drawing on many resources, including the past (Berman 1982:346). It is no coincidence that the rise of the public museum occurred at the same time, and as Preziosi (2002:31) has noted, one of its functions was to fabricate "a past that could be placed under systematic observation for use in (re)staging the present." Preziosi ties European antiquities and modernities together as "correlative co-constructions"; museums are intended to fabricate the past "for use in re-staging the present." Archaeology's claim to an authentic and objective version of the past linked the individual back to his or her essential roots; creating a national ethnic identity was served by archaeology, by the creation of museums and even later, in the twentieth century, by the promulgation of cultural preservation laws (Trigger 1984, 1995; Kristiansen 1992:13; Kohl and Fawcett 1995:3; Díaz-Andreu and Champion 1996:3; Stritch 2006:44). Archaeology's near obsession with documenting the increasing technological complexity of humanity as epitomized in Western culture contributed to the legitimi-zation—indeed, the naturalization—of nation-states and the global con-sequences that their dominant technologies and economies had on the rest of the world.

The dominance of modernity helped spawn the generalist model of *unilineal* evolutionism, exemplified by Morgan (1877), Tylor (1865), and Lubbock (1865), the latter's work in particular an attempt to chart the inescapable superiority of Western civilization. However, unilineal evo-lutionism increasingly clashed with the emergence of what became the culture history paradigm, which was partially engendered by the need for individual nation-states to establish their own *unique* past, their own culture history. The racist notions of Kossina (Trigger 1989:163–167) are but one ludicrous example of an increasingly nationalist archaeol-ogy, and at the very least there was an increasing preoccupation with specific culture histories. In Europe, Gordon Childe's (1925, 1926) quest for a specific European identity and Evans's own conceptualization of the Minoan past as the origins of European civilization are children of the same parents; Papadopoulos (2005) argues that Childe, as Ev-ans's "disciple," provided empirical evidence for Evans's initial model in operationalizing the archaeological culture (the intellectual debt owed by Childe to Evans [and Myres] is further explored by Andrew Sherratt [2006]). The tension between universal evolutionism and the emergence of a culture-historical paradigm aimed at creating specific cultural trajectories in specific areas,[6] for Evans at least, was resolved by his own take on Crete, in particular Knossos, as both the origins of a specific civilization (Greece) and the pedestal on which a whole stage of universal culture (Western civilization) could be built. Evans, therefore, knowingly or not, ended up with the best of both worlds. In the case of Knossos, excavations were intended to demonstrate, amongst other things, that Minoan civilization was the root of all subsequent West-ern culture. Yet, his reconstruction of Knossos simply mirrored British Victorian England (MacGillivray 2000; Hitchcock and Koudoumaris 2002:52; Lapatin 2002:51). In Evans's hands, the essential linearity of modernity became a circularity. He made the Cretan past like the modern present because it is the forerunner of all Western civilization (Silberman 1989:5). And how do we know that Minoan Crete was our forerunner? Just look at the similarities between the two. In putting the Minoans on the same evolutionary track as us, he created Minoan civilization as something that modern Europeans would want to claim as their own (Preziosi 2004:32; Papadopoulos 2005:88). Lowenthal (1985:378) captures the essence just right:

> Merely to know *about* the past is not enough; what is needed is a sense of intimacy, the intensely familiar interaction with antiquity that was a distinguishing and self-defining mark of European thought. To know the past in this fashion demands T.S. Eliot's perception 'not only of the pastness of the past, but of its presence'.

The control that foreigners exercised over Minoan archaeology in the nineteenth century has hardly been eradicated, for foreign archaeologists still have a great deal of intellectual control over Cretan archaeology. The pervasiveness of foreign influence is ironically demonstrated in an article by Hamilakis (2002b) pleading for a new direction for Minoan archaeology; of the sixty-six quoted authors who wrote on the subject, only twelve are actually Greek (it should also be noted, however, that more and more major projects are being run by Greek research teams). Foreign influence has been institutionalized by the antiquities permit system operated by the Greek government, which allocates blocks of permits to the various foreign schools (sixteen European states, the United States, Canada, and Australia have institutions in Athens, who then distribute the permits amongst their own competing researchers).[7] The Greek Archaeological Service conducts its own excavations, but with many of the major archaeological sites still "under contract" as it were to the major schools, it is difficult to escape the aura of academic colonialism that permeates Minoan archaeology. This had led to tensions between the foreign schools, the central Greek government, and the local population who too often see the field expeditions as foreign enclaves temporarily (or permanently) parachuted into their own private communities (Fotiadis 1993; Kardulias 1994b:382–383). Most of their work, certainly historically, has focused on what might be called *pure* research, rather than on such topics as the relationship between archaeological remains and contemporary communities, and criticism has been leveled at the Archaeological Service for tending simply to react to foreign proposals rather than proactively setting research agendas (Wallace 2005:58–59). This tension is also institutionalized in the state's archaeological bureaucracy; Kardulias (1994b:374) suggests that Greek archaeology, "which is deeply embedded in the state," actively works against foreign involvement for political and other reasons unrelated to the actual conduct of archaeological research. Kardulias (1994b:383) further notes how the political ambitions of Greek bureaucrats sometimes intrude into a decision-making process that he hopes should be an entirely objective scientific enterprise (cf. Zois [1990] for an opposing claim).

Academic Elitism .

The cultural elitism that characterized the nineteenth-century foreign domination of the island's archaeology can be further charted in the particular ways that the actual discipline of Minoan archaeology has been conducted. From its inception archaeology has been dominated by the mores of its practitioners, who have been for the most part middle or upper class. Research interests have often mirrored their own concerns and interests. Whether they emerged from the upper middle classes or the upper-class elite, these mores charted and celebrated the ever upward progress of humanity to more and more complex social organization, from savagery to civilization (cf. McGuire 1996). Shanks and Tilley (1987:63) baldly tie this into a not so unconscious affirmation of social hierarchy and inequality: "[e]galitarian societies dominated by the illiterate peasant lower classes are dull and boring, lacking in cultural achievement." The emphasis on culture as "a discourse of excellence . . . translates class and other forms of social inequality into *cultural capital*" (Shanks 2001:288). Consequently, considerably less attention has been paid to members of the so-called working class, in terms either of involving them in the overall archaeological project or of creating a past of interest to them (cf. Duke and Saitta 1998).

Evans was not particularly interested in identifying anybody in Minoan society who was unlike him: an educated and wealthy male (McEnroe 2002:69). Even though Evans recognized the presence of women at Knossos, I think it fair to say that his ideas on the role of women could still be considered patriarchal. Archaeological work during these early years emphasized the large palatial sites, and these sites and their exotic material culture dominated archaeological discourse, even if *lesser* sites were uncovered. Consider Medwid's (2000:160) judgment of David Hogarth (1862–1927), who excavated Phylakopi, the Dictaean Cave, Knossos, and Kato Zakro:

> A capable archaeologist, [he] was definitely limited by the outlook of his day. That is to say that he excavated monumental sites and sought artifacts which were aesthetically pleasing but discarded routine, everyday objects as "domestic rubbish."

Harriet Boyes Hawes found Gournia by accident, rather than with
any intent to excavate a town with only a provincial capital, and her
interpretation of the site was solidly in the prevailing Evans paradigm.
The decision to concentrate on the archaeology of a particular segment
of Minoan society sprang from their recognition that this was a civilization "comparable with those of the ancient Near East" (Dickinson
1994:2), but surely, also, also from their own individual backgrounds.[8]
Evans came from an extremely wealthy family; his grandfather was a
wealthy industrialist and his father a respected scholar, and so Evans
was able to buy Knossos for his own use (MacGillivray 2000), thereby
winning the competition between rival foreign archaeologists for rights
to the site, even though the Greek archaeologist, Minos Kolokairinos,
who had found the site was already working there (Hamilakis 2002a:2).[9]
Harriet Boyd Hawes, the excavator of Gournia, came from a solidly upper-middle-class family in Boston (five-story house, if you include the
basement, brother at Harvard, she at Smith, that sort of thing). Her
eminently readable biography, *Born to Rebel* (1992), written by her
daughter, Mary Allsebrook, traces the life of a rebel of sorts (for example, solo trips around Europe, first woman to lead an archaeological
dig in the Aegean, first woman to lecture at the Archaeological Institute
of America). She believed very strongly that the Cretans should retain
control over their own patrimony (Lapatin 2002:25).[10] The second generation of Minoan archaeologists also seems to have come from this
same middle- and upper-class social stratum. For example, John Devitt Stringfellow Pendlebury (to give him his full name), educated at
Winchester and Cambridge, was appointed curator of Knossos in 1929
(Branigan 2000:30). He was the son of the consulting surgeon to St
George's Hospital, London, and was financially independent as a result of a legacy from his grandfather, the shipowner Sir Thomas Devitt
(Powell 2001:61, 65). Letters to his father and the overall tone of work
at Knossos and its social atmosphere so lovingly described by Dilys
Powell in *The Villa Ariadne*, a virtual hagiography of Pendlebury (see
also Branigan's [2000] description of work on Crete between the two
world wars), reveal the upper-middle-class mores that permeated the
discipline here. John Pendlebury showed very little interest in the archaeological remains of sites other than the large palaces and the most
elaborate pottery (Dickinson 1994:2). There seems, then, an undoubted
link between the tone of Minoan archaeology during its formative years
and the individual background of its practitioners; the personal socioeconomic background of these archaeologists is surely not just coinci-
dental in trying to understand why they did what they did.

Perhaps we can still see traces of this elitism today, albeit in a different format, in, for instance, the individual pronunciation of Greek names and terms, with some scholars preferring the *Erasman* pronunciation and others the modern Greek form (*pithoi* vs. *pithi; Pylos* vs. *Peelos,* etc). This bifurcation can presumably be traced back to the nineteenth century when an "idealized Greece was defined as the starting point of Europeanness; access to it was through long training in the Greek language" (Morris 1994:20). Hamilakis (2006) refers to a "Creto-centricity" that allows Minoan archaeologists to assert their self-importance compared to those working on the mainland, to Cretan intellectuals who try to incorporate Crete into the Hellenic homeland, and even to locals who feel superior as it makes them antecedent and therefore superior to the other Greeks (regardless of the clear evidence that the line between them and the Minoans is hardly unbroken).

This structure of elitism is unfortunately common throughout the academy and is not restricted to Aegean archaeology. The result is that the production of knowledge is aimed primarily at a specialist audience. Major research institutions give greater kudos, in terms of tenure and promotion decisions, to faculty members who produce large quantities of articles and books aimed at other academics. Work aimed at the public is much less prestigious, and so what is offered to the public is often in the hands of nonspecialists.[11]

Archaeological Paradigms

The following discussion of the different approaches that Minoan archaeologists have employed is organized, if only for didactic purposes, around the three major paradigms of contemporary archaeology: culture history, processualism, and postprocessualism. The latter two paradigms in particular individually encompass a whole array of approaches, but each of them has a sufficiently unified set of assumptions and goals for it to be considered an individual paradigm. Each paradigm was introduced at different times in the development of the discipline, and each continues in contemporary archaeology, albeit in some cases in attenuated form.

The first paradigm, culture history, was introduced on both sides of the Atlantic in the late nineteenth century and was operationalized in the 1920s by scholars such as Childe in Europe and Kidder in the United States. This paradigm has the goal of organizing archaeological data into distinct time periods. This so-called chest-of-drawers approach

(Kohl 1981:91) relies on artifacts that serve as time markers, so that each time period can be easily recognized and, not coincidentally, represented in individual museum display cases. Often these time markers showed increasing technological sophistication (Thomson's three-age system, which divided prehistory into the Stone, Bronze, and Iron Ages inculcates this), so that the past is portrayed as representing the ever upward march of human progress. Each time period or archaeological culture could only be defined if internal temporal and cultural homogeneity were minimized. Minoan culture history is still largely dependent on Evans's tripartite division. There are still debates about the exact timing of these periods: for example, Betancourt's [1987] high chronology for the Late Minoan Period or the ongoing debate about the Thera eruption. The organization of the Minoan past is a model of increasing cultural advancement, culminating in the florescence of high Minoan Culture between 1700 and 1450 B.C. followed by a period of temporary decline (Platon [1962:22] went so far as to refer to "the decaying Minoan civilization"). Going beyond the Bronze Age, we see that Greek civilization finally picks itself up to culminate in the glories of fifth-century Athens.

While establishing a chronology might not seem to have particularly ideological ramifications, culture history is built on a number of assumptions and techniques that indirectly guide the observer into particular ways of thinking about the past and thereby the present. One example comes from how architecture and pottery—and this is the case on Crete—are very often used as the time markers in chronological models. Although not exclusively the preserve of the elite classes, very often those items of use in chronology building are. So, as an example, one chronology of Minoan Crete, described in Chapter 3, is based on changes to the architecture of the palaces. It is not necessary to go so far as to charge archaeologists with deliberately concentrating only on elite material culture: quite the contrary. Nevertheless, architecture and those items used in museums to chart the chronology of Crete unwittingly downplay mundane items of material culture.

Secondly, the creation of archaeological cultures is based on a normative assumption that at a particular time period, members of a culture are essentially all doing the same thing, making the same pottery, building the same tombs, and so on (with some recognition that it might be individual groups such as socioeconomic classes rather than whole societies that are the operative units). Hamilakis (2002a:11) has noted the paucity of debate in Minoan archaeology on "[i]nternal social contradictions and conflict, disruptions, and divergent developments in different parts of the island." However, is it so far-fetched to project from this cultural homogeneity a cultural stability with all that it implies about the past and the present; that social stability is what works, that such stability is the precondition for the glories of Minoan Crete? (Cf. Shanks and Tilley [1987:53] for an analogous criticism of the political implications of using systems analysis in archaeology.) Evans's concept of the peaceful Minoan thalassocracy is less moribund than some might think.

The second paradigm—processualism—was advocated as a scientific and objective way of studying and explaining the past. It was first introduced under the rubric of New Archaeology in the 1960s and in its myriad forms still holds considerable sway in the discipline. Despite its overt commitment to objective and value-free knowledge, this paradigm still has inescapably political dimensions to it that color any understanding of both the past and the present. I include in my discussion of this paradigm its intellectual forebear, nineteenth-century cultural evolutionism. I do this because each of them has parallel origins, both of them to a large extent being underwritten by state- and industry-supported science and both of them having similar political consequences.[12]

As already noted, archaeology and the creation of public museums in the nineteenth century was part, consciously or not, of the larger modernist project of establishing the legitimacy of the modern state and the natural dominance of scientific knowledge. Evans too was influenced by unilinear cultural evolutionists like Lubbock, although he had to temper that influence with the increasing influence of the newly emergent culture-historical paradigm. Evans set the tone for the essentialist evolutionary model that still guides Minoan archaeology; that is, the inexorable rise of society to more and more complex forms. Comparatively few Aegean archaeologists have asked the converse: if the rise of the state is indeed inexorable, why did it not occur in many more places? (Lewthwaite [1983] is an exception.)

The reliance on the evolutionary model was furthered by Renfrew's contributions to Aegean archaeology in the 1970s, in particular *The Emergence of Civilization: The Cyclades and the Aegean in the Third Millennium* (Renfrew 1972). This work is a landmark in Aegean archaeology, not just for providing a synthesis of a very complicated area, but for introducing to the Aegean the principles of the New Archaeology, such as systems analysis and neo-evolutionism. The new archaeology was heavily influenced by Leslie White's application of the second law of thermodynamics to human society. Much of his work is replete with nouns, verbs, and adjectives that would be quite at home in the unilinear texts of the nineteenth century. For instance (my emphasis): *"culture* advances *as the amount of energy harnessed per capita increases"* (1959:56); "an increase in the amount of energy harnessed will . . . carry culture *forward"* (1959:57); "energy is the dynamic, living force that animates cultural systems and develops them *to higher levels and forms"* (1959:37). Elman Service (1962) and Marshall Sahlins (1968) introduced the four-fold evolutionary system of social organization (band, tribe, chiefdom, and state) that *operationalized* White's model. Underlying their system was an assumption that "the greater selective fitness of technologically advanced societies ensured that progress characterized cultural change as a general feature of human history" (Trigger 1989:292). Renfrew (1972:364) acknowledged the definitional problems with both the terms *state* and *chiefdom*, sometimes calling the Bronze Age Aegean societies chiefdoms and sometimes chiefdom-states. The essential assumption—cultural evolution toward greater technological and social complexity—underpinned later Aegean studies. For example, Cherry (1984:18) stated that "[i]t is widely accepted that distinctive polities of an institutional complexity sufficient to consider as 'states' first appeared in the Aegean shortly after c. 2000 B.C." Given this conclusion, the issue devolved to whether the rise of the state was endogenous or exogenous (Cherry 1984:21), and whether it was a gradual process or one of stability interrupted by short qualitative changes similar to the biological model of punctuated equilibrium (cf. Haggis 2002:121).

Although the neo-evolutionary model still holds considerable sway in Minoan archaeology, some archaeologists have rejected both the terminology of chiefdom and state, and indeed the very model itself. Borrowing from McGuire (1983), Hamilakis (2002a:14) advocates the concepts of heterogeneity (the distribution of population among social groups) and inequality (the differential access to resources between these groups) as a means of understanding the basic structure of Minoan society as something other than a rigid hierarchical social structure, thereby allowing much greater fluidity and impermanence in the power of ruling factions. This approach, he believes, will provide a more convincing picture of what went on during the second millennium and give us a better understanding of what changes took place and why.

There is, therefore, a good case for arguing that Minoan society did *not* get more complex during the second millennium. Certainly, there is little evidence for greater heterogeneity, one of the criteria for this development. However, because of the influence of the neo-evolutionary model on Minoan archaeology, the past is presented as indicating just that. An unholy alliance has been unwittingly created between cultural ideology and intellectual paradigms. Thus, the lower classes of

Minoan life are less well studied because that has been the historical tone of Minoan archaeology (an ideological sin of omission) and because neo-evolutionary archaeology tells us the inexorable development of human society is to greater complexity, even though on both empirical and epistemological grounds the argument has no validity when applied to Minoan culture in the first place (an intellectual sin of commission).

Postprocessual approaches emerged in the early 1980s with the potential to rectify the sins of our fathers. They have become more popular on the European side of the Atlantic and have *captured* some existing approaches to archaeology such as gendered and indigenous archaeologies. Unfortunately, the potential offered by postprocessualism for engaging hitherto neglected constituencies has not been fully realized, either. First, I think it fair to say that postprocessual archaeology is still doggedly middle class, and there has often been a gap between the democratizing rhetoric of postprocessual archaeology and the language and vocabulary of its presentation (cf. Duke and Saitta 1998). Secondly, the postprocessual project has devoted considerably less effort to class issues than to the creation, say, of feminist or even indigenous archaeologies (Duke and Saitta [1998] have offered reasons why this is the case). Thirdly, we are still a long way from the creation of a truly democratic archaeology. Indeed, there is an inherent self-contradiction in too much postprocessual archaeology. For example, a shrine at Catal Huyuk for Mother Goddess worshippers (Hodder 1999:195)? There is nothing wrong with opening up the site to a new constituency—indeed it should be celebrated. But who possibly could afford even to go to Catal Huyuk? Only the leisured and wealthy—the traditional constituency of archaeology. No, archaeology is still too much a profoundly leisured exercise, and all of us who practice it are implicated in this elitist structure to a greater or lesser extent. So while, to use Bakhtin's terms (1981, 1984), we may have achieved a heteroglossia in archaeology (i.e., the same authoritarian message presented in different forms of expression), we have not achieved a true polyphony (or multivocality), marked by "the autonomy and strength of the voices, which are represented as engaged in open-ended dialogue where ultimate values are in play but necessarily cannot be finalized" (Joyce 2002:11).

The recognition of the ideological dimension to the interpretation of the Minoan past was discussed by Bintliff (1984:38), whose analysis of the context of Arthur Evans's work concluded that "a more important factor [than new finds' forcing reinterpretations] is the outlook of the archaeologist *on his own world*, subsequently *reflected* in the messages of reinforcement he seeks and claims to recover from the world of the Past." Yet we are allowed to ask how much headway this approach has made. This can be gauged by MacGillivray's (2000) *Minotaur*, a comprehensive exposé of Evans's work at Knossos and how his interpretation of Minoan society was influenced heavily by his own background. For in this book, MacGillivray (2000:9), a highly respected Minoan archaeologist, touts his work as "a radical departure from the common view of how archaeology and archaeologists work." Recent edited volumes by Hamilakis (2002b) and Hamilakis and Momigliano (2006) show the potential for postprocessualist approaches (I trust that Hamilakis, Momigliano, and their contributors will not overly object to being placed under this rubric). The goal of Hamilakis (2002b) is to excavate the intellectual strata of Minoan archaeology in order to isolate the political and ideological underpinnings of knowledge production. Papers in Hamilakis and Momigliano (2006) examine how the concept of "The Minoans" has been produced and consumed by different publics since the late nineteenth century. Unfortunately the revisionist approach embodied in these works is that it is not survey- or excavation-oriented. And in a region where sites and material culture still seem to be the primary focus of investigation, as much dictated by the need for chronology building as anything else, the implications of this important volume might not seep through the discipline as much as might be necessary.

State Control of Archaeology

From its very beginnings as a modern nation-state, Greece saw the political potential to controlling the past by announcing its commitment to protecting its antiquities (Kotsakis 1991:65), and almost as soon as Crete was able to move away from Ottoman sovereignty, the island's national assembly passed laws controlling the export of its antiquities; only objects "unsuitable for the museums" could be exported (Lapatin 2002:20). The Greek Archaeological Service, the central organization charged with protecting the archaeological heritage of the country, was established in 1833 and since 1971 has been a department of the Ministry of Culture. Its primary mandate is the excavation, protection, and management of the archaeological sites and museums in its jurisdiction. The service fulfills its mandate through regional administrative units called ephorates, of which there are three on Crete, located at Iraklio, Agios Nikolaos, and Chania.

The control that the central government tries to exercise over the past is no better demonstrated than in their policies regarding site docents. Although individuals are free to visit archaeological sites unescorted, only qualified guides who have attended the Schools for Tour Guides are allowed to lecture groups on the sites and Greek history.[13] The schools are one arm of the Organization of Tourism Education and Training, which operates under the Greek Ministry of Development (www.ste.edu.gr/uk/ste_uk.htm), and are located in Athens and Thessaloniki and sometimes Iraklio, Corfu, Mytilini, and Rhodes. The course is two and half years in length and consists of theoretical courses and educational visits and trips. The primary emphasis of these schools is to educate the guides in Greek history. The seven core modules for the course are all about the Greek past: prehistoric archaeology; classic archaeology; Byzantine archaeology; history of art; ancient history; Byzantine history, modern history. Topics like botany, geography, geology, and first aid are part only of the secondary module.

The schools are oriented to the tourist market. Of the six aims listed on the school's website, one in particular stands out:

> [T]he contribution to the fulfillment of the goals of the tourism
> policy, focusing on the improvement of the Greek tourism
> product competitiveness and the dynamic development of
> the tourism business.

It therefore should come as no surprise, given this agenda, that the school tries to control what the guides say. Each year the guides are required to take a refresher course where amongst other things they are advised on what to stress and what political topics to avoid. The goal presumably is to ensure that tourists are not in any way drawn into controversial topics. The past remains sanitized.

Economics

In 2003 Greece received 14,179,999 foreign tourists, a figure larger than its resident population (and this after the 9/11 attacks had caused a worldwide tourist recession), placing it in fifteenth position in the worldwide tourism "league table." Consequently, revenue from tourism is a fundamentally important component of the overall Greek economy, providing 15 percent of total gross domestic product.[14] In 2005, this resulted in total tourist receipts of $13,391 million (www.euromonitor.com). Employment from tourism is about 10 percent of the total work force (6.1 percent direct; 3.9 percent indirect) and is provided not just in the direct service industries of hotels and restaurants but in the shops that are geared totally to fulfilling tourist needs, and which are open only during the summer months.

Crete has been part of this economic tourist boom. The island was in serious economic trouble until the advent of mass tourism in the 1970s, its economy largely dependent on traditional farming practices, especially in the mountains (Pettifer 1994:75–76.) In the 1950s, approximately 70 percent of Cretans were subsistence farmers. By the early 1980s, tourism had grown at a faster rate than elsewhere in Greece, and the service industry now generates between 30 and 50 percent of the island's gross regional product per year (Kousis 1996:221; www.cretadomus.com). The island, whose resident population is about 700,000, now receives anywhere from two to three million tourists a year, most of them arriving by air at Nikos Kazantsakis Airport just outside Iraklio. Based on arrivals at this airport, most foreign tourists are British or German.[15] Although socioeconomic statistics for tourists are not available, a tourist stay on the island is about 20 percent higher than the country's average and would suggest that visitors tend to be more at the upper end of the socioeconomic spectrum. This is confirmed by a sample survey of six hundred visitors to Knossos and Iraklio museum (Apostolakis and Jaffry 2005:231–232). Of the 243 responses 47.9 percent described themselves as "professional and managerial." Almost 90 percent had a secondary or higher education. Income levels ranged from € (Euros) 0–10,000 (8.3 percent), € 10,001–30,000 (29.2 percent), € 30,001–50,000 (42.0 percent), to € 50,001 or more (20.5 percent). Forty two percent of the tourists are families with children, 38 percent are couples, and 20 percent singles. Forty-nine percent fall into the 18–35 year old category, 22 percent into the 36–45 year old category, and 18 percent into the 46–60 year old category. It is significant that approximately 80–85 percent come as part of a package tour, which consists of air fares, accommodations, and very often a number of tours (optional) to archaeological sites and museums. This perhaps explains why Knossos experiences such a high visitation year after year (close to a million visitors annually). These figures suggest, therefore, two conclusions. First, on Crete a remarkably high percentage of the visitors actually do end up on one or more archaeological sites. Second, that because of the demographic and familial status of the visitors, the presentation of the past caters to middle-class tastes and mores. Indeed, it became clear from Apostolakis and Jaffry's sample survey that visitors would be quite happy to pay a larger entrance fee at Knossos and Iraklio Museum, if that meant fewer visitors. They concluded that "higher entrance fees would favour those who place the highest value on the heritage experience and the attractions by generating higher revenue to cover the operating costs" (Apostolakis and Jaffry 2005:241–242).

The importance of archaeological tourism to the Greek economy is not seen, however, just in the statistics, revealing though these may be. The impact must also be seen in the various private enterprises that have sprung up around the major and sometimes not so major sites. These enterprises comprise the expected tourist souvenir shops that sell not just replicas of the treasures recovered from the sites and the whole range of tourist needs such as suntan lotion, postcards, and so on, but also offer in some instances free parking, in the hopes that one will feel "guilt" and stop to savor and then buy the goods on sale.

Archaeology and the Local Constituency

The paradox of the political control of the Greek—and the Minoan—past is how that very same past has been used as a tool to confirm both a colonialist presence and a nationalist heritage. Greece stresses "those elements of the archaeological record that serve to make of the past a coherent, unified theme, that begins with some golden age and continues unbroken to the present; archaeology is a tool in the effort to maintain the integrity of the ethnos and its great legacy" (Kardulias 1994b:382). The net result is that the inhabitants of Crete were largely excluded from the creation of that past, and even today their participation in that past can be argued to be on others' terms rather than their own.

This exclusion traces its roots to the very beginnings of Minoan archaeology. The benevolent attitude of early archaeologists to the Cretan past did not always extend to its modern inhabitants. Cretan scholars at the turn of the century embraced the "modernist myths" to validate the ideological incorporation of the island into the rest of Greece and Europe (Hamilakis 2006:149). It is not the Cretans alone who have been treated in this way. Modern Greeks in general find themselves between an ideological rock and a hard place, and many nineteenth-century travelers to Greece saw modern Greeks as caught between the East and the West, receiving illumination from neither of them (Peckham 1999:168).[16] This was caused partly by the long-standing effects of nineteenth-century philhellenism, which had "driven a wedge between ancient and modern as surely as the Orientalists had done" (Morris 1994:23). It is little wonder that in the eyes of many, modern Greeks (including, of course, Cretans) just couldn't stand comparison with their golden past. David Hogarth, the early Minoan archaeologist, saw the modern Greeks as having fallen from the ideals of their ancestors because of the corruption of the Orient (McEnroe 2000.04), as did his contemporary, Virginia Woolf (Peckham 1999:175). Modern Greeks or their culture, it appears, just weren't worth the effort of getting to know.

Evans certainly had a contradictory attitude toward modern Cretans. On the one hand, he celebrated Minoan culture and he certainly wanted Crete to be free of Ottoman oppression, although whether this was fueled as much by anti-Islamism as by philhellenism is a source of controversy. On the other hand, he had a proprietary (at the very least) attitude toward Minoan remains. He was quite happy to purchase pieces from locals and he illegally removed artifacts from various sites on the island (Lapatin 2002:18–19); although he criticized relic hunters, he apparently felt that he was above local laws. He was convinced that modern Cretans were not the best stewards of their ancient past. MacGillivray (2000) has complained that Evans showed a disdain that bordered on contempt for contemporary Cretans and their culture. He eschewed Cretan food and wine in favor of imported French varieties, and the erection of the Edwardian *Villa Ariadne* sent an unblinking message to the local inhabitants of exactly where this Englishman stood on their social scale and is a good example of Gosden's assertion (2004) that colonialism must be explained in terms of how material culture helped destabilize indigenous values. Perhaps MacGillivray's criticism, however, is a little overdone. For example, Ronald M. Burrows (1907:22), Professor of Greek at University College, Cardiff, and the author of *The Discoveries in Crete and Their Bearing on the History of Ancient Civilization*, congratulated Evans on his wonderful picnics "under the olive trees, with the red wine from *Mount Ida* [my italics]." Or perhaps MacGillivray was right, and Burrows just was not on the A-list, not worthy of the imported wines. The surviving photographs of Evans, whether taken on Crete or back home in England, epitomize the English Victorian gentlemen with all the accompanying stereotypical prejudices. Indigenous inhabitants were seen as interesting elements of the cultural backdrop with no real understanding of the sites in their own backyard (McGillivray 2000).[17] Evans's paternalistic sense of *noblesse oblige* has been called racist by some (cf. McEnroe 2002:70). Whether or not he was an outright racist is probably not an issue worth pursuing. Although the terms that Evans used to describe Africans depicted on Minoan art, for example, do come straight from the "language of nineteenth century racism and colonialism," this was something to be expected of someone of Evans's class and age (McEnroe 1995:16–17). It might be best not to judge too harshly by viewing nineteenth century mores through the spectacles of twenty-first century morals. We can probably place his derogatory remarks about "Red Indians" in the same light (Evans 1908:9, cited in Papadopoulos 2005:97).

Even if modern Cretans are no longer judged not to have lived up to the standards of their illustrious forebears, their exclusion from how their island's past was constructed still leaves them in an ambivalent position. This is not to say that they do not connect with the past at particular levels of awareness and consciousness (cf. Hamilakis 2006), although knowing about an archaeological site and its past is not the same as having control, complete or otherwise, over how that knowledge is constructed and entered into contemporary discourse. Indeed, it is the discourse between the local and the national that makes for a complicated palimpsest of social negotiation and contestation. This is no better exemplified than by an incident that took place in 1979 (Hamilakis and Yalouri 1996). The Greek central government tried to take Minoan treasures from the Iraklio museum for a series of exhibitions in various foreign cities, including Paris and New York. Crowds of Cretans demonstrated to prevent their removal. Several reasons could be posited for this behavior: (1) economic self-interest; (2) the recognition of a separate Cretan identity that was being usurped by the central government in Athens; (3) resistance to American hegemony in the eastern Mediterranean (Hamilakis and Yalouri 1996:126). The reasons are perhaps less significant than the fact that the demonstrations took place at all. For the demonstrations showed that despite the centuries of overweening control by foreign oppressors, economic weakness, the discipline of archaeology, tourism, and a central bureaucracy in Athens, the inhabitants of Crete still are connected to the past and see it as a tool of use in their present struggles. In a further reading of this event, Hamilakis (2006:159) has drawn a homology between the artifacts and persons, in that the Cretans tried to stop the objects from being "abducted" and forced to leave their "home." Thus, "antiquities become persons that are incorporated into the broader national family."

Knossos does have social value to contemporary Cretans (Papadopoulos 2005:120), if not in same way as its use during the 1950s, when it served "rather as a recreation site [for locals] than an ancient site" (Myers 1951:7, cited in Papadopoulos 2005:118). Myers's own prickliness in this statement is reflective surely of his professional interest in the site. Simandaraki (2006) has recently shown how the teaching of Minoan history to Cretan schoolchildren by such means as sailing

Figure 5.1 *House with faux Minoan façade*

a reconstructed vessel allows a connection to the past. However, she points out too that this past is sanitized, with no reference allowed to Minoan practices like possible human sacrifice. Hamilakis (2006), relying in part on Lenakake's recent ethnographic research, points out that the identity with the Minoan past is at least partially dependent on the Cretan's proximity to one of the major sites or his or her reliance on tourism for income. One individual returning to Crete after many years' absence "connected" with the Minoan past because only absence made him appreciate how archaeologically important Crete was. The motifs of Minoan architecture are a popular choice for residences on the island. The faux Minoan façade found on the house in Figure 5.1 is not unique. Bar and hotel owners alike decorate their public rooms with pictures that are either drawn impressionistically from Minoan palaces or are more accurate visual representations. One beachfront nightclub in Rethymno until recently had an interior entrance that was covered with various copies of the Knossos frescoes. Clearly the images of the Minoan past are known and utilized in different ways. Yet while we might acknowledge that contemporary Cretans do connect with their island's Minoan past, I would argue that it does not do so at the intensity of a structural nostalgia a là Herzfeld (1991:75), where the past is made to represent the embodiment of superior qualities.

Making the Minoan past the past of *all* Europeans denies Cretans any semblance of truly local ownership,[18] and indeed, it is hard not to conclude that local inhabitants have little to no control over what of their island's past is constructed and passed onto the tourists who descend for a week or two a year. Most of these decisions are not made at the local level but in Athens, and the halls of academia, certainly not in the local villages of the island. For example, no new buildings are allowed around Knossos that are not considered "appropriate" (Solomon 2006), although local inhabitants resist what they see as a bureaucratic intrusion into their own community (an analogous situation is how the historic past of Rethymno's old town has become part of the contestation between local and state interests).

Given that only an extended ethnographic study would capture all the nuances that would show, let alone explain, how the Minoan past exists in the Cretan present, the following should be considered only as impressionistic vignettes. I found that sometimes the knowledge about the Minoan past did not extend beyond generalities. One lady with whom I conversed at Eleftherna was vaguely aware of the local site, but opined that everything was old and then shrugged, as if to say that there wasn't much else anyone needed to know. One Rethymniot I met was not aware of the existence of Kato Zakro or Agia Triada, but had heard of Knossos and Phaistos. Even his knowledge of Knossos was fairly generalized, and I found this to be the same with other restaurateurs and shopkeepers I talked to. At Phourni, even the attendant feigned disinterest in the site until I mentioned Sakellarakis, the excavator of the site. Then his eyes lit up. Others I chatted with did not have a deep knowledge of the Minoan past beyond the existence of Knossos. This did not surprise me; indeed it should probably be expected. The details of Stonehenge or Avebury, for example, do not seem particularly well known to most people I've met in Britain, and I could perhaps say the same thing about many—perhaps most—people in the Four Corners area of the southwestern United States. Despite their proximity to Mesa Verde and Chaco Canyon, they do not always know the specifics of the sites. Yet, the examples provided earlier suggest that the Minoan past is part of many Cretans' identity, and professional archaeologists should not hold nonprofessionals to unrealistic standards of esoteric knowledge.

The relationship between local Cretans and the Minoans' past is paradoxically similar to what happens when archaeological sites are privatized, for although Minoan sites are owned by the state, the relationship between the state and Cretans does not allow for local control. Palumbo (2006:37) draws a clear distinction between a market-oriented cultural heritage exploitation and a socially focused and community-owned cultural heritage use. Palumbo's (2006:38) specific distinctions between the two are worth listing in full:

	Market Approach	*Social Approach*
Economy	Seeks immediate return	Economic value not most important
Values	Favors those that can be sold to the public	Local interpretations of high importance
Context	A monument with little relationship with its surroundings	Part of a cultural continuum with its surroundings
Management	Needs continuous reinvestment to maintain competitiveness	Balances use and conservation
Main Objective	Tourism	Public good
Local community	Is in service to cultural heritage exploitation	Local community participates in conservation
Effects	Exploitation degrades the local resource	Use adds value to the resource
Sustainability	Nonsustainable	Sustainable

It can be concluded, therefore, that although the archaeological sites and museums are putatively "owned" by the public, control of them and the knowledge they contain is strictly controlled in favor of nonlocal, primarily economic interests.

In this chapter I have unpacked what I consider to be the main influences on the construction of the Minoan past and its appropriation by and integration into different contemporary cultural strategies, in particular the presentation of the Minoan past to the tourists who come to Crete each year. It is now time to suggest how this study can contribute to wider disciplinary issues. This is the purpose of the final chapter of this study.

NOTES

1. Modern nationalism is about two hundred years old (Kristiansen 1992:14), and in recognizing the existence of other states ensured that states entered into multiple relationships of cultural inferiority and superiority with each other (cf. Smith [1971] for an alternative view on the history of nationalism).

2. An example shows the complexity of this issue. In the summer of 2004, while visiting Crete, I saw a blond northern European girl wearing the traditional Sfakian male headscarf fringed in front with the black cloth droplets representing the tears shed for freedom. She shouldn't be wearing that, I thought. It's not right. But someone, Greek probably, even Cretan, had mass-produced it (you can find the headscarves in the tourist shops) and sold it to her. So, I presume they thought it alright. Who, I concluded, am I to defend Crete's heritage?

3. The human side of this revolt is vividly portrayed in Nikos Kazantsakis's (1973) autobiography, *Report to Greco*.

4. Yet, the nationalistic rivalry between the schools is exemplified in an offhanded comment made by Ronald M. Burrows in his 1907 book, *The Discoveries of Crete*. The book, written by the Professor in Greek at the University of Cardiff, is at times a virtual paean to Evans's work. Although he feels forced to comment that Evans does not leave his excavations "clean and well-ordered," Burrows cannot help but knock the French in the same sentence for "the disgracefully untidy state in which [they] have left Delos [which] shows that even so much is not to be expected of all explorers" (Burrows 1907:22).

5. At least one reviewer (Jenkyns 2001) has called into question the insistence by MacGillivray and others (e.g. McEnroe 2002) of Evans' essential racism.

6. The increasing resistance to unilinealism was paralleled in American anthropology, which under the influence of the American Franz Boas rejected evolutionism in favor of a historically particularistic ethnography. As the professional anthropologist of the early twentieth century became a tribal specialist, so did the archaeologist increasingly become a site and regional specialist (Harris 1968:676)

7. The Greek government grants a small number of archaeological field permits for both survey and excavation per year per school, regardless of the school's size, and these are then opened to internal competition (Kardulias 1994b:380). Three permits per school are available for survey, three for excavation, and three for collaboration with an official Greek partner (Papadopoulos 2003:32; Wallace 2005:58). The system results not just from the long history of foreign schools conducting archaeological research, often accompanied by a sense of long-term rights to research on a site or in a region (Wallace 2005:57–58). It also arises from the simple fact of their generally having more money available for research than Greek archaeologists.

8. The cult of personality that Evans initiated (Powell 2001)—for example, he has a hotel in Iraklio named after him—spread to later generations. The same town also has a Ventris Street, named after the decipherer of Linear B. And although the aura of John Pendlebury, Evans's successor at Knossos, and his romantic death in the early hours of the German invasion is waning, it is hard to imagine many archaeologists today getting the mix of scholarly respect and human adoration that he received in Platon's eulogy:

"Dear friend, Crete will preserve your memory among her most sacred treasures. The soil which you excavated with the archaeologist's pick and enriched with a warrior's blood will shelter you with eternal gratitude."

The aura is not quite extinguished, as indicated by a recent exhibition on Pendlebury's life at the village of Tzermiado in the Lasithi region (Wallace 2005:62).

0. Looting of archaeological sites was probably quite common in the nineteenth century. As early as the 1830s Pashley (1837:76, vol. II) commented on *excavations* at the site of Phalasarna by treasure hunters.

10. Unfortunately, she was not immune to the sexism rampant at the time. After leaving Smith and teaching at a number of secondary schools, she was awarded a fellowship to begin graduate studies at the American School of Classical Studies in Athens. She was prevented, however, from actually participating in archaeological fieldwork by her professors, who encouraged her to become a librarian instead (*Athena Review* 2003c).

11. A refreshing exception is Joseph Shaw's (2006), *Kommos: A Minoan Harbor Town and Greek Sanctuary in Southern Crete.* Clearly intended for the nonspecialist, it is not, however, patronizing, but rather brings the reader into the exciting and intellectually stimulating world of archaeological discovery.

12. I am grateful to my colleague Kathy Fine for the particular turn of phrase in this sentence. In a number of works, Alice Kehoe (1993, 1998) has convincingly teased out the connection between processualism and scientism.

13. Nationals of other countries are prohibited from guiding at archaeological sites for commercial companies, although they can lecture to their groups in hotels. Non-Greek nationals are allowed to talk on site and in museums to university groups, so long as they have obtained the necessary permit from the Greek Ministry of Culture.

14. Further economic statistics are found in:
    - www.cia.gov/publications/factbook/geos/gr www.euromonitor.com/factfile.aspx?country = GR)
    - www.gnto.gr
    - www.creta-ingo.gr
    - www.cretadomus.com.

15. Greek tourists who overnight comprise only one in ten of the total tourist population, a figure far lower than the 25 percent for the rest of Greece as a whole.

16. Consider these comments: "Greece may be unique in the degree to which the country as a whole has been forced to play the contrasted roles of *Ur-Europa* and humiliated Oriental vassal at one and the same time" (Herzfeld 1989:19); "The Greeks were made to embrace a romanticized version of their classical identity" (Lowenthal 1994:307).

17. However, it is difficult not to feel some degree of warmth for someone like Evans, whose greatest compliment about Richard Seager, his contemporary in Minoan archaeology, was that he was "the most *English* American I have ever known" (Lapatin 2002:2).

18. Denying local inhabitants control over their past is not unique to Crete. A similar denial has occurred in some parts of Australia over aboriginal rock art (Bowdler [1988], cited in Byrne 1991).

CHAPTER SIX

The Nexus of the Past

As more and more countries discover the foreign revenue to be gained from tourism, so do those countries turn to their archaeological and historical pasts to entice foreign visitors, whether it be through the private-sector heritage industry or government-controlled or -sponsored agencies. As tourism becomes an increasingly global phenomenon and as the past is co-opted more and more into the tourism industry, archaeologists concerned with the social and political ramifications of their profession can plough fertile ground by examining precisely how messages about the past are conveyed to the touring public through this co-optation, and thereby how those same messages can legitimize or destabilize particular contemporary ideologies. Such examinations also answer the call for more anthropological interest in the effect of cultural contact on the guest communities (in this case, tourists) rather than on the host cultures themselves (in this case, Crete and its Minoan past), important though the latter may be. The increased attention that the public is paying to the archaeological past may be welcomed by the discipline, but it comes at a price: archaeology is faced with a Faustian bargain (Russell 2006:22) "in its relationship to modernity, especially with regard to the role of images of the past in heritage and tourism industries."

The nexus between the archaeological past of Crete and the tourists who provide a major investment in the island's economy has been the particular subject of this study. I have tried to demonstrate that in this particular instance a single past has been, and continues to be, projected and that this past has repercussions for how archaeological tourists view both that past and their own present. My reading is based on my own particular cultural background, and I have concluded that the past projected at tourist sites on Crete essentializes the metanarrative of social inequality in the West. While local constituencies may try to push back for their own reasons (as Solomon's [2006] study exemplifies), they are severely undergunned, fighting as they are not just a modern heritage bureaucracy but thirty-five hundred years of Western civilization and its interpretation. Examining the total range of information on the Minoan past that is available to tourists to the island indicates how overwhelming the message about that past has become. It scarcely allows for the sorts of contestation of the past that other students of heritage have sought to identify.

A recurrent theme of this book is that the past is not an objective entity but rather is constructed in response to a number of factors. Figure 6.1 provides a schematic understanding of this, in particular the nexus between the present and the Minoan past. The Minoan past projected to tourists is the result (1) of the academic community and its members' own ideological and research predilections; (2) the need for the West to claim first classical Greece and then Minoan Crete as the origins of western civilization; (3) the modern Greek state, which appropriated Greek history as a tool of the state in order to legitimize its own existence in the nineteenth century and to make it an equal partner (even if the attempt was unsuccessful) with other contemporary European states. This past has been further appropriated with the state's blessing and financial support as a major marketing tool in the selling of Crete to foreign tourists. Thus, there is a mutually enforcing relationship between the past and the modern economic necessities of the island. The economic importance of the tourist industry to the modern Greek state is large and has been noted in this study. The tourist industry uses only certain parts and motifs of the Cretan past. Tourists are fed a diet of a glorious Minoan monarchy with lavish palaces, beautiful frescoes, and a peaceful and happy populace. Knossos is offered to tourists as the primary, and sometimes only, port of call.

It does not have to be this way. However, it would require archaeologists and museum managers to alter fundamentally their perceptions of what the public wants to see on display. And it is an insufficient response to suggest that the "pretty" things are all the public wants, for how will we know if this is the case unless professionals actively attempt to draw the public into a meaningful dialogue about *all* of Minoan life? I remain struck by the differences in how Gournia and Knossos are treated. Even if Gournia (fifty miles from Iraklio, but only fifteen from Agios Nikolaos) or Kato Zakro (seventy-five miles from Iraklio) are too far away from the major hotel complexes to justify a large-scale expenditure of resources on visitor amenities (which might conversely attract more visitors were they provided), smaller sites like Tylissos (less than ten miles from Iraklio) or Vathypetro (ten miles) can be visited easily. Such sites are important and can offer much of interest about aspects of Minoan life. I have written elsewhere (Duke 2006:86):

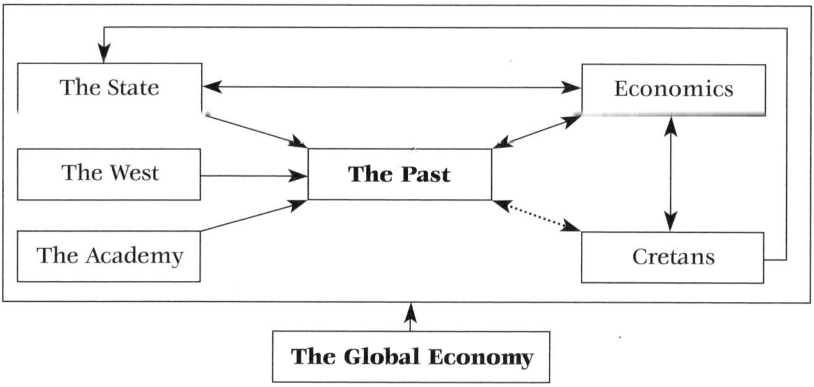

Figure 6.1 *The nexus between the present and the Minoan Past*

Consider an alternative scenario. Gournia, located on the Gulf of Mirabello, can be seen as an ordinary Minoan 'working-class' town, despite the presence of a small palace vainly copying the larger palaces to the west. If Gournia were the metaphor by which tourists understood the Minoan past, then a totally different past would be known. Here the past is important for the works and lives of ordinary 'working-class' men and women. The elite fade into obscurity. A different site provides a different metaphor, which provides a different past and thereby a different understanding of the present.

Archaeology was conceived as a middle-class enterprise and it has been—and continues to be—redolent with middle-class mores, ideologies, and interests. If archaeology is to continue down the path to becoming a more socially and politically aware discipline, it must make itself available to as wide a segment of society as possible, perhaps more than its practitioners initially feel comfortable with. Constructing an engendered archaeology caused the first brick to fall in the wall that isolated archaeology as a middle-class, white, male-dominated society. Drawing Native Americans and other indigenous groups into archaeological discourse was a painful exercise for many archaeologists, but in the long run it has been beneficial in that it has expanded the discipline's relevance beyond its traditional constituencies. Making our discipline relevant to as wide a constituency as possible is our responsibility as state-sponsored academics. Given the importance of the past in attracting tourists, the nexus between tourism and the past is a fruitful area for examining the expansion of the discipline. If this present study has contributed to this examination, then it will have served its purpose.

REFERENCES CITED

Akeroyd, Anne V.
  1981   Comments on *Tourism as an Anthropological Subject* by Dennison Nash. *Current Anthropology*. 22:468–469.

Allsebrook, Mary
  1992   *Born to Rebel: The Life of Harriet Boyd Hawes*. Oxbow Books, Oxford.

Ames, Michael
  1992   *Cannibal Tours and Glass Boxes*. University of British Columbia Press, Vancouver (2nd edition).

Anderson, Benedict
  1983   *Imagined Communities: Reflections on the Origin and Spread of Nationalism*. Verso Editions, New York.

Andreadaki-Vlasaki, Maria
  2002   Are We Approaching the Minoan Palace of Khania? In *Monuments of Minos: Rethinking the Minoan Palaces,* pp. 157–166. Edited by Jan Driessen, Ilse Schoep, and Robert Laffineur. Aegaeum 23. Annales d'Archéologie Égéenne de l'Université de Liège et UT-PASAP.

Apostolakis, Alexandros and Shabar Jaffry
  2005   Heterogeneous Preferences for Greek Heritage Attractions. *Tourism Economics* 11:225–245.

Appadurai, Arjun
  1981   The Past as a Scarce Resource. *Man* 16:201–219.
  1986   Introduction: Commodities and the Politics of Value. In *The Social Life of Things: Commodities in Social Perspective*, pp. 3–63. Edited by Arjun Appadurai. Cambridge: Cambridge University Press, Cambridge.

Arnold, J. K. Davies and S. Ditchfield (editors)
  1998   *History and Heritage: Consuming the Past in Contemporary Culture*. Donhead, Shaftesbury.

Ashmore, Wendy and Robert J. Sharer
  2000   *Discovering Our Past: A Brief Introduction to Archaeology*. Mayfield Publishing, Mountain View, CA.

Athena Review
  2003a Bronze Age Writing on Crete: Hieroglyphs, Linear A, and Linear B. *Athena Review* 3. On-line version *www.athenapub.com*.
  2003b Sir Arthur Evans and the Excavation of the Palace at Knossos. *Athena Review* 3. On-line version *www.athenapub.com*.
  2003c Harriet Boyd and the Excavation of Gournia. *Athena Review* 3. On-line version *www.athenapub.com*.
  2003d Discoveries at Khania in Western Crete: An Interview with Maria Andreadaki-Vlasiki. *Athena Review* 3. On-line version www.athena pub.com.

Baedeker's Mediterranean Islands
  1984 Prentice Hall, Englewood Cliffs, N.J.

Bakhtin, M. M.
  1981 *Dialogic Imagination: Four Essays.* University of Texas Press, Austin.
  1984 *Problems of Dostoevsky's Poetics.* University of Minnesota Press, Minneapolis.

Barrett, John
  2000 Comments on Wilkie and Bartoy's "A Critical Archaeology Revisited." *Current Anthropology* 41:761–762.

Barthes, Roland
  1987 *Mythologies.* Hill and Wang, New York (first edition, 1957).

Benavides, O. Hugo
  2004 *Making Ecuadorian Histories. Four Centuries of Defining Power.* University of Texas Press, Austin.

Bennet, John
  2000 Linear B and Linear A. In *Cretan Quests: British Explorers, Excavators and Historians*, pp. 129–137. Edited by Davina Huxley. The British School at Athens, London.

Bennett, Tony
  1988 Museums and 'the People'. In *The Museum Time-Machine*, pp. 63–85. Edited by Robert Lumley. Routledge, London.

Berlitz Discover Greece
  1996 Berlitz Publishing Company, Princeton, NJ

Berlitz Travellers Guide to Greece
  1992 Berlitz Publishing Company, New York.

Berman, Marshall
  1982 *All That Is Solid Melts into Air: The Experience of Modernity.* Simon and Schuster, New York.

Betancourt, Philip
  1987 Dating the Aegean Late Bronze Age with Radiocarbon. *Archaeometry* 29:45–49.
  2002 Who Was in Charge of the Palaces? In *Monuments of Minos: Rethinking the Minoan Palaces,* pp. 207–211. Edited by Jan Driessen, Ilse Schoep, and Robert Laffineur. *Aegaeum* 23. Annales d'Archéologie Égéenne de l'Université de Liège et UT-PASAP.

Betancourt, Philip and Nanno Marinatos
　1997　The Minoan Villa. In *The Function of the "Minoan Villa,"* pp. 91–98. Edited by Robin Hägg. Paul Åströms Förlag.

Biers, William R.
　1996　*The Archaeology of Greece.* Cornell University Press, Ithaca NY (2nd edition).

Binford, Lewis
　1989　*Debating Archaeology.* Academic Press, San Diego.

Bintliff, John L.
　1984　Structuralism and Myth in Minoan Studies. *Antiquity* LVIII:33–38.

Bodnar, J.
　1992　*Remaking America: Public Memory, Commemoration, and Patriotism in the Twentieth Century.* Princeton University Press, Princeton.

Boissevain, Jeremy
　1996　Introduction. In *Coping with Tourists*, pp. 1–26. Edited by Jeremy Boissevain. Berghahn Books, Providence, RI.

Boorstin, Daniel J.
　1964　*The Image: A Guide to Pseudo-Events in America.* Harper and Row, New York.

Böröcz, József
　1992　Travel Capitalism: The Structure of Europe and the Advent of the Tourist. *Comparative Studies in Society and History* 34:708–741.
　1996　*Leisure Migration: A Sociological Study on Tourism.* Elsevier Science, Tarrytown, NY.

Bowdler, S.
　1988　Repainting Australian Rock Art. *Antiquity* 62:517–523.

Branigan, Keith
　2000　Between the Wars. In *Cretan Quests: British Explorers, Excavators and Historians*, pp. 28–33. Edited by Davina Huxley. The British School at Athens, London.

Broodbank, Cyprian
　2004　Minoanization. *Proceedings of the Cambridge Philological Society* 50:46–91.

Broodbank, Cyprian and Thomas F. Strasser
　1991　Migrant Farmers and the Neolithic Colonization of Crete. *Antiquity* 65:233–245.

Bruner, Edward M.
　2005　*Culture on Tour: Ethnographies of Travel.* University of Chicago Press, Chicago.

Burns, Peter M.
　1999　*An Introduction to Tourism and Anthropology*, Routledge, London.

Burrows, Ronald M.
　1907　*The Discoveries in Crete.* John Murray, London.

Byrne, Denis
    1991   Western Hegemony in Archaeological Heritage Management.
            History and Anthropology. 5:269–276.

Cadogan, Gerald
    1992a   Ancient and Modern Crete. In *The Aerial Atlas of Ancient Crete*, pp.
            27–29. Edited by J. Wilson Myers, E.E. Myers, and G. Cadogan
            Thames and Hudson, London.
    1992b   Gournia. In *The Aerial Atlas of Ancient Crete*, pp. 104–111. Edited by
            J. Wilson Myers, E.E. Myers, and G. Cadogan. Thames and Hudson,
            London.
    1992c   Knossos. In *The Aerial Atlas of Ancient Crete*, pp. 124–147. Edited by
            J. Wilson Myers, E.E. Myers, and G. Cadogan. Thames and Hudson,
            London.
    1992d   Vathypetro. In *The Aerial Atlas of Ancient Crete*, pp. 282–285. Edited
            by J. Wilson Myers, E.E. Myers, and G. Cadogan. Thames and
            Hudson, London.

Cameron, Pat
    2003   *Blue Guide: Crete.* A&C Black, London.

Campbell, Robert
    1988   Busman's Holiday—or the Best Surprise Is No Surprise. *Kroeber
            Anthropological Society Papers*: 12–19.

Castañeda, Quetzil E.
    1996   *In the Museum of Maya Culture: Touring Chichen Itza.* University of
            Minnesota Press, Minneapolis.

Chambers, Erve
    2000   *Native Tourism: The Anthropology of Travel and Tourism.* Waveland
            Press, Prospect Heights, NJ.

Cherry, John F.
    1984   The Emergence of the State in the Prehistoric Aegean. *Proceedings
            of the Cambridge Philological Society* 30:18–48.

Childe, V. Gordon
    1925   *The Dawn of European Civilization.* Kegan Paul, London.
    1926   *The Aryans: A Study of Indo-European Origins.* Kegan Paul, London.

Clifford, James and George E. Marcus (editors)
    1986   *Writing Culture: The Poetics and Politics of Ethnography.* University
            of California Press, Berkeley.

Cohen, Erik
    1974   Who Is a Tourist? A Conceptual Clarification. *The Sociological Review*
            22:527–555.
    1988   Authenticity and Commodization in Tourism. *Annals of Tourism
            Research* 15:371–386.
    1995   Contemporary Tourism—Trends and Challenges: Sustainable
            Authenticity or Contrived Post-Modernity? In *Change in Tourism:
            People, Places, Processes*, pp. 12–29. Edited by Richard Butler and
            Douglas Pearce. Routledge, London.

Collins, Michael
    2004 *The Likes of Us.* Granta Books, London.
Cottrell, Leonard
    1967 *The Lion Gate.* Pan Books, London.
Crawshaw, Carol and John Urry
    1997 Tourism and the Photographic Eye. In *Touring Cultures: Transformations of Travel and Theory,* pp. 176–195. Edited by Chris Rojek and John Urry. Routledge, London.
Crick, Malcolm
    1985 "Tracing" the Anthropological Self: Quizzical Reflections on Fieldwork, Tourism and the Ludic. *Social Analysis* 17:71–92.
    1989 Representations of International Tourism in the Social Sciences: Sun, Sex, Sights, Savings and Servility. *Annual Review of Anthropology* 18:307–344.
Cullen, Tracey
    2001 Voices and Visions of Aegean Prehistory. In *Aegean Prehistory: A Review,* pp. 1–18. Edited by Tracey Cullen. *American Journal of Archaeology Supplement 1.* Archaeological Institute of America, Boston.
Dann, Graham
    1995 A Sociolinguistic Approach towards Changing Tourist Imagery. In *Change in Tourism: People, Places, Processes,* pp. 114–136. Edited by Richard Butler and Douglas Pearce. Routledge, London.
    1996 *The Language of Tourism: A Sociolinguistic Perspective.* Cab International, Oxford.
Dann, Graham and Erik Cohen
    1996 Sociology and Tourism. *The Sociology of Tourism: Theoretical and Empirical Investigations,* pp. 301–314. Edited by Yiorgos Apostolopoulos, Stella Leivadi, and Andrew Yiannakis. Routledge, London.
Dartmouth.edu
    1997a Lesson 14: Late Minoan Painting and Other Representational Art: Pottery, Frescoes, Steatite Vases, Ivories, and Bronzes. www.dartmouth.edu/ history/ bronze_age/ lessons/14.html.
    1997b Lesson 15: Minoan Religion. www.dartmouth.edu/history/bronze_age/ lessons/15.html.
Davaras, Costis
    1976 *Guide to Cretan Antiquities.* Eptalofos S.A., Athens.
    1992 Chamaizi. In *The Aerial Atlas of Ancient Crete,* pp. 78–81. Edited by J. Wilson Myers, E.E. Myers, and G. Cadogan. Thames and Hudson, London.
Davis, Jack L.
    2001 Review of Aegean Prehistory I: The Islands of the Aegean. In *Aegean Prehistory: A Review,* pp. 19–76. Edited by Tracey Cullen. *American Journal of Archaeology Supplement 1.* Archaeological Institute of America, Boston.

Day, Peter M. and Maria Relaki
  2002 Past Factions and Present Fictions: Palaces in the Study of Minoan
      Crete. In *Monuments of Minos: Rethinking the Minoan Palaces,*
      pp. 217–234. Edited by Jan Driessen, Ilse Schoep, and Robert
      Laffineur. *Aegaeum* 23. Annales d'Archéologie Égéenne de
      l'Université de Liège et UT-PASAP.

Dening, Greg
  1992 *Mr Bligh's Bad Language: Passion, Power and Theatre on the Bounty.*
      Cambridge University Press, Cambridge.

Díaz-Andreu, Margarita and Tomithy Champion
  1996 Nationalism and Archaeology in Europe; an Introduction. In
      Nationalism and Archaeology in Europe, pp. 1–23. Edited by
      Margarita Díaz-Andreu and Timothy Champion. Westview Press,
      London.

Dickinson, Oliver
  1994 *The Aegean Bronze Age.* Cambridge University Press, Cambridge.

Discover Greece
  1996 Berlitz Publishing, Princeton, N.J.

Dorling Kindersley. The Greek Islands
  1997 Dorling Kindersley Publications, London.

Driessen, Jan
  1999 The Archaeology of a Dream: The Reconstruction of Minoan Public
      Architecture. *Journal of Mediterranean Archaeology* 12(1):121–127.
  2002 "The King Must Die." Some Observations on the Use of Minoan
      Court Compounds. In *Monuments of Minos: Rethinking the Minoan
      Palaces,* pp. 1–14. Edited by Jan Driessen, Ilse Schoep, and Robert
      Laffineur *Aegaeum* 23. Annales d'Archéologie Égéenne de
      l'Université de Liège et UT-PASAP.
  2003 The Court Compounds of Minoan Crete: Royal Palaces or
      Ceremonial Centers? *Athena Review* 3. On-line version
      www.athenapub.com.

Driessen, Jan and Colin F. Macdonald
  1997 The Troubled Island: Minoan Crete Before and After the Santorini
      Eruption. *Aegaeum* 17.

Driessen, Jan, Ilse Schoep, and Robert Laffineur (editors)
  2002 *Monuments of Minos: Rethinking the Minoan Palaces. Aegaeum* 23.

Dufour, R.
  1978 Des Mythes du Loisir/Tourisme Weekend: Aliénation ou Libération?
      Cahiers du Tourisme, série C., no. 47. Annales d'Archéologie
      Égéenne de l'Université de Liège et UT-PASAP.

Duke, Philip
  1993 Forests, Trees, and Archaeological Vision: A Parable from Chimney
      Rock. In *The Chimney Rock Archaeological Symposium*: pp. 91–94. Ed.
      J. M. Malville and G. Matlock. *General Technical Report RM-22,* United
      States Department of Agriculture, Fort Collins, CO.

2006   Knossos as Memorial, Ritual, and Metaphor. In "Archaeology and European Modernity: Producing and Consuming the 'Minoans'", pp. 79–88. Edited by Yannis Hamilakis and Nicoletta Momigliano. Special volume of *Creta Antica 7*. Bottega d'Erasmo, Aldo Ausilio, Padua.

Duke, Philip, Randall McGuire, Dean Saitta, Paul Reckner, and Mark Walker
2005   The Colorado Coalfield War Archaeological Project: Archaeology Serving Labor. In *Preserving Western History*. Ed. by Andrew Gulliford: pp. 32–43. University of New Mexico Press, Albuquerque.

Duke, Philip and Dean Saitta
1998   An Emancipatory Archaeology for the Working Class. *Assemblage* 4. *www.shef.ac.uk/assem/4.*

Duke, Philip and Michael C. Wilson
1995   Introduction: Postprocessualism and Plains Archaeology. In *Beyond Subsistence: Plains Archaeology and the Postprocessual Critique*, pp. 1–16. Edited by Philip Duke and Michael C. Wilson. University of Alabama Press, Tuscaloosa.

Duncan, James and Derek Gregory
1999   Introduction. In *Writes of Passage: Reading Travel Writing*, pp. 1–13. Edited by James Duncan and Derek Gregory. Routledge, London.

Durrell, Lawrence
1978   *The Greek Islands*. The Viking Press, New York.
1996   *Prospero's Cell*. Marlowe and Co., New York. (1st edition 1945)

Evans, Arthur
1908   The European Diffusion of Pictography and Its Bearings on the Origin of Script. In *Anthropology and the Classics: Six Lectures Delivered Before the University of Oxford*, pp. 9–43. Edited by R.R. Marett. Oxford University Press, Oxford.
1921   *The Palace of Minos. Volume I.* Macmillan, London.

Fabian, Johannes
1983   *Time and the Other: How Anthropology Makes its Object*. Columbia University Press, New York.

Fair, Lansing
2004   Opportunities for Presenting Sites Better: A City Planner's Perspective. Paper presented at the Annual Meeting of the Archaeological Institute of America, San Francisco.

Fletcher, Roland
1989   The Messages of Material Behavior: A Preliminary Discussion of Non-Verbal Meaning. In *The Meaning of Things. Material Culture and Symbolic Expression*, pp. 33–40. Edited by Ian Hodder. Unwin Hyman, London.

Fodor's Guide to Greece
1999   Fodor's Travel Publications, New York.

Fotiadis, Michael
    1993   Regions of the Imagination: Archaeologists, Local People, and the
            Archaeological Record in Fieldwork, Greece. *Journal of European
            Archaeology* 1:151–170.

Freely, John
    1988   *Crete.* New Amsterdam Books, New York.

Gans, Herbert J.
    1962   *The Urban Villagers.* The Free Press, New York.

Gathercole, Peter and David Lowenthal (editors)
    1994   *The Politics of the Past.* Routledge, London.

Gifford, John A.
    1992   The Geomorphology of Crete. In *The Aerial Atlas of Ancient Crete*,
            pp. 17–25. Edited by J. Wilson Myers, E.E. Myers, and G. Cadogan.
            Thames and Hudson, London.

Goodison, Lucy and Christine Morris
    1999   Beyond the Great Mother. The Sacred World of the Minoans. In
            Ancient Goddesses, pp. 113–132. Edited by Lucy Goodison and
            Christine Morris. The University of Wisconsin Press, Madison.

Gosden, Chris
    2004   *Archaeology and Colonialism: Cultural contact from 5000 BC to the
            Present.* Cambridge University Press, Cambridge.

Graburn, Nelson H.H.
    1977   The Museum and the Visitor Experience. In *The Visitor and the
            Museum*, pp. 5–44. Edited by Linda Draper. Prepared for The
            American Association of Museums Annual Conference.
    1989   Tourism: The Sacred Journey. In *Hosts and Guests: The
            Anthropology of Tourism*, pp. 21–36. Edited by Valene L. Smith.
            University of Pennsylvania Press, Philadelphia.

Graburn, Nelson H.H. and Roland S. Moore
    1994   Anthropological Research on Tourism. In *Travel, Tourism, and
            Hospitality Research: A Handbook for Managers and Researchers*, pp.
            233–243. Edited by J.R. Brent Richie and Charles R. Goeldner.
            John Wiley and Sons, New York (2nd edition).

Greenwood, Davydd J.
    1989   Culture by the Pound: An Anthropological Perspective on Tourism
            as Cultural Commoditization. In *Hosts and Guests: The Anthropology
            of Tourism*, pp. 171–185. Edited by Valene L. Smith. University of
            Pennsylvania Press, Philadelphia.

Gregory, Derek
    1999   Scripting Egypt. Orientalism and the Cultures of Egypt. In *Writes
            of Passage: Reading Travel Writing*, pp. 164–184. Edited by James
            Duncan and Derek Gregory. Routledge, London.

Habermas, Jurgen
    1973   *Legitimation Crisis.* Heinemann, London.

Haggis, D.C.
  2002 Integration and Complexity in the Late Prepalatial Period: A
       View from the Countryside in Eastern Crete. In *Labyrinth Revisited:
       Rethinking Minoan Archaeology*, pp. 120–142. Oxbow Books, Oxford.

Hamilakis, Yannis
  1996 Wine, Oil and the Dialectics of Power in Bronze Age Crete: A
       Review of the Evidence. *Oxford Journal of Archaeology* 15:1–32.

  1998 Consumption Patterns, Factional Competition and Political
       Development in Bronze Age Crete. *Bulletin of the Institute of Classical
       Studies at the University of London* 42:233–234.

  1999 Food Technologies/Technologies of the Body: The Social Context
       of Wine and Oil Production and Consumption in Bronze Age Crete.
       World Archaeology 31.

  2002a What Future for the 'Minoan' Past? Re-Thinking Minoan
       Archaeology. In *Labyrinth Revisited: Rethinking Minoan Archaeology*,
       pp. 2–28. Oxbow Books, Oxford.

  2002b *Labyrinth Revisited: Rethinking Minoan Archaeology*. Oxbow Books,
       Oxford. (editor)

  2002c Too Many Chiefs? Factional Competition in Neopalatial Crete. In
       Monuments of Minos: Rethinking the Minoan Palaces, pp. 179–199.
       Edited by Jan Driessen, Ilse Schoep, and Robert Laffineur. *Aegaeum*
       23. Annales d'Archéologie Égéenne de l'Université de Liège et
       UT-PASAP.

  2002d The Past as Oral History: Towards an Archaeology of the Senses.
       In *Thinking through the Body: Archaeologies of Corporeality*, pp.
       121–136. Edited by Yannis Hamilakis, Mark Pluciennik, and Sarah
       Tarlow. Kluwer Academic, New York.

  2006 The Colonial, the National and the Local: Legacies of the "Minoan"
       Past. In "Archaeology and European Modernity: Producing and
       Consuming the 'Minoans'," pp. 145–162. Edited by Yannis Hamilakis
       and Nicoletta Momigliano. *Creta Antica* 7. Bottega d'Erasmo, Aldo
       Ausilio, Padua.

Hamilakis, Yannis and Nicoletta Momigliano (eds.)
  2006 Archaeology and European Modernity: Producing and Consuming
       the 'Minoans'. Special volume of *Creta Antica* 7. Bottega d'Erasmo,
       Aldo Ausilio, Padua.

Hamilakis, Yannis and Eleana Yalouri
  1996 Antiquities as Symbolic Capital in Modern Greek Society. *Antiquity*
       70:117–129.

Harris, Marvin
  1968 *The Rise of Anthropological Theory*. Thomas Y. Crowell, New York.

Hawes, Charles Henry and Harriet Boyd Hawes.
  1911 *Crete: The Forerunner of Greece*. Harper and Brothers, New York
       (2nd edition).

Herzfeld, Michael
  1989 *Anthropology through the Looking-Glass: Critical Ethnography in the
       Margins of Europe*. Cambridge University Press, Cambridge.

1991   *A Place in History: Social and Monumental Time in a Cretan Town.*
Princeton University Press, Princeton.

Hitchcock, Louise
1999   Postcards from the Edge: Towards a Self-Reflexive Reconstruction
of Knossos. *Journal of Mediterranean Archaeology* 12(1):128–133.
2003   Understanding the Minoan Palaces. *Athena Review* 3. On-line
version *www.athenapub.com.*

Hitchcock, Louise and Paul Koudounaris
2002   Virtual Discourse: Arthur Evans and the Reconstructions of the
Minoan Palace at Knossos. In *Labyrinth Revisited: Rethinking
Minoan Archaeology*, pp. 40–58. Oxbow Books, Oxford.

Hobsbawm, Eric and Terence Ranger (editors)
1983   *The Invention of Tradition.* Cambridge University Press, Cambridge.

Hodder, Ian
1986   *Reading the Past.* Cambridge University Press, New York.
1999   *The Archaeological Process: An Introduction,* Blackwell Publishers,
Oxford.
2003   Archaeological Reflexivity and the "Local" Voice. *Anthropological
Quarterly* 76:55–69.

Honey, Martha
1999   *Ecotourism and Sustainable Development: Who Owns Paradise?*
Island Press, Washington, D.C.

Howard-Malverde, Rosaleen
1997   Introduction. Between Text and Context in the Evocation of
Culture. In *Creating Context in Andean Cultures*, pp. 1–18. Edited by
Rosaleen Howard-Malverde. Oxford University Press, Oxford.

Howell, Benita J.
1994   Weighing Risks and Rewards of Involvement in Cultural Conservation
and Heritage Tourism. *Human Organization* 53:150–159.

Hoyau, Philippe
1988   Heritage and 'the Conserver Society': The French Case. In *The
Museum Time-Machine*, pp. 27–35. Edited by Robert Lumley.
Routledge, London.

Insight Guide to Crete (Discovery Channel)
n.d.   Langenscheidt Publishers, Maspeth, NY.

Jenkyns, Richard
2001   The Labyrinth of Arthur Evans. *New York Review of Books.*
November 1.

Joyce, Rosemary A.
2002   *The Languages of Archaeology.* Blackwell, Oxford.

Kardulias, P. Nick
1994a   Paradigms of the Past in Greek Archaeology. In *Beyond the Site:
Regional Studies in the Aegean Area*, pp. 1–23. Edited by P. Nick
Kardulias. University Press of America, Lanham, MD.

1994b Archaeology in Modern Greece: Bureaucracy, Politics, and Science. In *Beyond the Site: Regional Studies in the Aegean Area*, pp. 373–387. Edited by P. Nick Kardulias. University Press of America, Lanham, MD.

Kazantzakis, Nikos
1973 *Report to Greco*. Faber and Faber, London (first English edition 1965).

Kehoe, Alice B.
1993 Processual and Postprocessual Archaeology: A Brief Critical Review. In *Beyond Subsistence: Plains Archaeology and the Postprocessual Critique*, pp. 19–27. Edited by Philip Duke and Michael C. Wilson. University of Alabama Press, Tuscaloosa.
1998 *The Land of Prehistory*. Routledge, New York.

Kelleher, Michael
2004 Images of the Past: Historical Authenticity and Inauthenticity from Disney to Times Square. *CRM: The Journal of Heritage Stewardship* 1:6–19.

Kincaid, Jamaica
1989 *A Small Place*. Penguin Books, Harmondsworth, England.

Klynne, Allan
1998 Reconstructions of Knossos: Artists' Impressions, Archaeological Evidence and Wishful Thinking. *Journal of MediterraneanArchaeology* 11:206–229.

Kohl, Philip L.
1981 Materialist Approaches in Prehistory. *Annual Review of Anthropology* 10:89–118.

Kohl, Philip L. and Clare Fawcett
1995 Archaeology in the Service of the State: Theoretical Considerations. In *Nationalism, Politics, and the Practice of Archaeology*, pp. 3–18. Edited by Philip L. Kohl and Clare Fawcett. Cambridge University Press, Cambridge.

Kotsakis, Kostas
1991 The Powerful Past: Theoretical Trends in Greek Archaeology. In *Archaeological Theory in Europe*, pp. 65–90. Edited by Ian Hodder. Routledge, London.
1999 Comment on Y. Hamilakis, 'La trahison des archéologues.' *Journal of Mediterranean Archaeology* 12:96–98.

Kousis, Maria
1996 Tourism and the Family in a Rural Cretan Community. In *The Sociology of Tourism: Theoretical and Empirical Investigations*, pp. 219–232. Edited by Yiorgos Apostolopoulos, Stella Leivadi, and Andrew Yiannaki. Routledge, London.

Kristiansen, Kristian
1992 'The Strength of the Past and its Great Might': An Essay on the Use of the Past. *Journal of European Archaeology* 1:3–32.

Lakoff, George
    1996   *Moral Politics*. University of Chicago Press, Chicago.
Lancaster, Osbert
    1947   *Classical Landscape with Figures*. John Murray, London.
Lanfant, Marie-Françoise
    1995   Introduction. In *International Tourism: Identity and Change*, pp. 1–23.
            Edited by Marie-Françoise Lanfant, John B. Allcock, and Edward M.
            Bruner. Sage Publications, Thousand Oaks, CA.
Lapatin, Kenneth
    2002   *Mysteries of the Snake Goddess: Art, Desire, and the Forging of History*.
            De Capo Press, Cambridge, MA.
La Rosa, Vincenzo
    1992a   Ayia Triada. In *The Aerial Atlas of Ancient Crete*, pp. 70–77. Edited
            by J. Wilson Myers, E.E. Myers, and G. Cadogan. Thames and
            Hudson, London.
    1992b   Phaistos. In *The Aerial Atlas of Ancient Crete*, pp. 232–243. Edited
            by J. Wilson Myers, E.E. Myers, and G. Cadogan. Thames and
            Hudson, London.
    1997   La "Villa Royale" de Haghia Triada. In *The Function of the "Minoan
            Villa,"* pp. 79–89. Edited by Robin Hägg. Paul Åströms Förlag.
Layton, Robert
    1989   *Who Needs the Past? Indigenous Values and Archaeology*. Unwin
            Hyman, London.
Leone, Mark
    1987   Rule by Ostentation: The Relationship between Space and Sight in
            Eighteenth-Century Landscape Architecture in the Chesapeake
            Bay Region of Maryland. In *Method and Theory for Activity Area
            Research*, pp. 604–633. Edited by Susan Kent. Columbia University
            Press, New York.
    1988   The Georgian Order as the Order of Merchant Capitalism in
            Annapolis, Maryland. In *The Recovery of Meaning: Historical
            Archaeology in the Eastern United States*, pp. 235–262. Edited by
            Mark P. Leone and P.B. Potter, Jr. Smithsonian Institution Press,
            Washington, DC.
Lewthwaite, James
    1983   Why Did Civilization Not Emerge More Often? A Comparative
            Approach to the Development of Minoan Crete. In *Minoan Society*,
            pp. 171–183. Edited by O. Krzyskowska and L. Dixon. Bristol
            Classical Press, Bristol.
Lonely Planet. Greece
    2000a   Lonely Planet Publications, Melbourne.
Lonely Planet. Greek Islands
    2000b   Lonely Planet Publications, Melbourne.
Lowenthal, David
    1985   *The Past is a Foreign Country*. Cambridge University Press, Cambridge.

1994 Conclusion: Archaeologists and Others. In *The Politics of the Past*, pp. 302–314. Edited by Peter Gathercole and David Lowenthal. Routledge, London.

Lubbock, John
1865 *Pre-historic Times, as Illustrated by Ancient Remains, and the Manners and Customs of Modern Savages*. Williams and Norgate, London.

Lumley, Robert
1988 Introduction. In *The Museum Time-Machine*, pp. 1–23. Edited by Robert Lumley. Routledge, London.

MacCannell, Dean
1973 Staged Authenticity: Arrangements of Social Space in Tourist Settings. *American Journal of Sociology* 79:589–603.
1976 *The Tourist: A New Theory of the Leisure Class*. Schocken Books, New York.
1992 *Empty Meeting Grounds*. Routledge, London.

MacConnell, Brian E.
1989 Mediterranean Archaeology and Modern Nationalism: A Preface *Revue des Archéologues et Historiens d'Art de Louvain*. 22:107–113.

Macdonald, Colin
2003 The Palace of Minos at Knossos. *Athena Review* 3. On-line version *www.athenapub.com*.

MacDonald, Sharon
1998 Exhibitions of Power and Powers of Exhibition: An Introduction to the Politics of Display. In *The Politics of Display: Museums, Science, Culture*, pp. 1–24. Edited by Sharon MacDonald. Routledge, London.

MacGillivray, Alexander
2000 *Minotaur: Sir Arthur Evans and the Archaeology of the Minoan Myth*. Hill and Wang, New York.
2002 Memories of a Minotaur. In *Monuments of Minos: Rethinking the Minoan Palaces*, pp. 213–216. Edited by Jan Driessen, Ilse Schoep, and Robert Laffineur. *Aegaeum* 23. Annales d'Archéologie Égéenne de l'Université de Liège et UT-PASAP.
2003 Return to the Labyrinth: A Clew to the Function of the Minoan Palaces. *Athena Review* 3. On-line version *www.athenapub.com*.

MacGillivray, J. Alexander and L. Hugh Sackett
1992 Palaikastro. In *The Aerial Atlas of Ancient Crete*, pp. 222–232. Edited by J. Wilson Myers, E.E. Myers, and G. Cadogan. Thames and Hudson, London.

MacLean, Rory
2004 *Falling for Icarus*. Penguin books, London.

Malaby, Thomas
2003 Spaces in Tense: History, Contingency, and Place in a Cretan City. In *The Usable Past: Greek Metahistories*, pp. 171–189. Edited by K.S. Brown and Yannis Hamilakis. Lexington Books, Lanham.

Marx, Karl
  1986 *Capital. Volume I.* Penguin Books, New York (original 1867).
McEnroe, John C.
  1995 Sir Arthur Evans and Edwardian Archaeology. *Classical Bulletin* 71:3–18.
  2002 Cretan Questions: Politics and Archaeology 1898–1913. In *Labyrinth Revisited: Rethinking 'Minoan' Archaeology*, pp. 59–72. Edited by Yannis Hamilakis. Oxbow Books, Oxford.
McGuire, Randall
  1983 Breaking Down Cultural Complexity: Inequality and Heterogeneity. *Advances in Archaeological Method and Theory* 6:91–142.
  1996 Why Complexity Is Too Simple. In *Debating Complexity*, pp. 23–30. Edited by P.C. Dawson and D.T. Hanna. Archaeology Association, University of Calgary.
McNeal, Richard A.
  1991 Archaeology and the Destruction of the Later Athenian Acropolis. *Antiquity* 65:49–63.
Medwid, Linda M.
  2000 *The Makers of Classical Archaeology: A Reference Work.* Humanity Books, New York.
Merriman, Nick
  1989 Heritage from the Other Side of the Glass Case. *Anthropology Today* 5:14–15.
  1996 Understanding Heritage. *Journal of Material Culture.* 1:377–386.
Michelin Tourist Guide to Greece
  1998 Tourism Department, Michelin Tyre PLC, Watford.
Miller, Henry
  1941 *The Colossus of Maroussi.* New Direction Books, New York.
Miller, Michelle A.
  2003 Introduction: Courtyard Complexes and the Labyrinth of Minoan Culture. *Athena Review* 3. On-line version www.athenapub.com.
Minh-ha, Trinh T.
  1989 *Woman, Native, Other.* Indiana University Press, Bloomington.
Moody, Jennifer
  1997 The Cretan Environment: Abused or Just Misunderstood? In *Aegean Strategies: Studies of Culture and Environment on the European Fringe*, pp. 61–77. Edited by P. Nick Kardulias and Mark T. Shutes. Rowman and Littlefield, Lanham, MD.
Morgan, Lewis Henry
  1877 *Ancient Society.* Holt, New York.
Morris, Christine and Alan Peatfield
  2002 Feeling through the Body: Gesture in Cretan Bronze Age Religion. In *Thinking through the Body: Archaeologies of Corporeality*, pp. 105–120. Edited by Yannis Hamilakis, Mark Pluciennik, and Sarah Tarlow. Kluwer Academic, New York.

Morris, Ian
  1994   Archaeologies of Greece. In *Classical Greece: Ancient Histories
         and Modern Archaeologies*, pp. 8–17. Edited by Ian Morris.
         Cambridge University Press, Cambridge.

Moser, Stephanie
  2001   Archaeological Representations: The Visual Conventions for
         Constructing Knowledge about the Past. In *Archaeological Theory
         Today*, pp. 262–283. Edited by Ian Hodder. Polity Press, Cambridge.

Myers, J.L.
  1951   The Palace of Knossos: British Estate Offered to the Greek
         Government. *The Times* 14th July, 1951:7.

Nash, Dennison
  1981   Tourism as an Anthropological Subject. *Current Anthropology.*
         2:461–481.
  1996   *Anthropology of Tourism.* Pergamon Press, Tarrytown, New York.

Nash, Dennison and Valene L. Smith
  1991   Anthropology and Tourism. *Annals of Tourism Research* 18:12–25.

Niemeier, Wolf-Dietrich
  1997   The Origins of the Minoan "Villa" System. In *The Function of the
         "Minoan Villa,"* pp. 15–19. Edited by Robin Hägg. Paul Åströms Förlag.

Nilsson, M.P.
  1950   *The Minoan-Mycenaean Religion.* C.W.K. Gleerup, Lund.

Palaima, Thomas
  2003   Archaeology and Text: Decipherment, Translation, and
         Interpretation. In *Theory and Practice in Mediterranean Archaeology:
         Old World and New World Perspectives*, pp. 45–73. Edited by John
         K. Papadopoulos and Richard M. Leventhal. Cotsen Advanced
         Seminars 1. The Cotsen Institute of Archaeology.

Palumbo, Gaetano
  2006   Privatization of State-Owned Cultural Heritage: A Critique of Recent
         Trends in Europe. In *Of the Past, for the Future: Integrating
         Archaeology and Conservation*, pp. 35–39. Edited by Neville Agnew
         and Janet Bridgland. The Getty Conservation Institute, Los Angeles.

Palyvou, Clairy
  2003   Architecture and Archaeology: The Minoan Palaces in the Twenty-
         First Century. In *Theory and Practice in Mediterranean Archaeology:
         Old World and New World Perspectives*, pp. 205–233. Edited by John
         K. Papadopoulos and Richard M. Leventhal. Cotsen Advanced
         Seminars 1. The Cotsen Institute of Archaeology.

Papadopoulos, John K.
  2003   Engaging Mediterranean Archaeology: Old World and New World
         Perspectives. In *Theory and Practice in Mediterranean Archaeology:
         Old World and New World Perspectives*, pp. 3–32. Edited by John K.
         Papadopoulos and Richard M. Leventhal. Cotsen Advanced
         Seminars 1. The Cotsen Institute of Archaeology.
  2005   Inventing the Minoans: Archaeology, Modernity and the Quest for
         European Identity. *Journal of Mediterranean Archaeology* 18:87–149.

Pashley, Rober
    1837   *Travels in Crete, Volumes I and II*. John Murray, London (Dion. K.
           Karavias Reprints).

Patrik, Linda
    1985   Is There an Archaeological Record? *Advances in Archaeological
           Method and Theory* 8:27–62.

Patterson, Thomas C.
    1986   The Last Sixty Years: Toward a Social History of Americanist
           Archeology Transformations of Travel and Theory in the United
           States. *American Anthropologist* 88:7–26.

Peatfield, Alan
    2000   Minoan Religion. In *Cretan Quests: British Explorers, Excavators
           and Historians*, pp. 138–150. Edited by Davina Huxley. The British
           School at Athens, London.

Peckham, Robert Shannan
    1999   The Exoticism of the Familiar and the Familiarity of the Exotic.
           Fin-de-siècle Travelers to Greece. In *Writes of Passage: Reading
           Travel Writing*, pp. 164–184. Edited by James Duncan and Derek
           Gregory. Routledge, London.

Pelon, Olivier, Jean-Claude Poursat, René Treuil, and Henri Van Effenterre
    1992   Mallia. In *The Aerial Atlas of Ancient Crete*, pp. 175–185. Edited by
           J. Wilson Myers, E.E. Myers, and G. Cadogan. Thames and Hudson,
           London.

Pettifer, James
    1994   *The Greeks: The Land and People since the War*. Penguin Books, London.

Platon, N.
    1962   *A Guide to the Archaeological Museum of Heraclion*. Heraclion, Crete.
    1992   Zakro. In *The Aerial Atlas of Ancient Crete*, pp. 292–301. Edited by
           J. Wilson Myers, E.E. Myers, and G. Cadogan. Thames and Hudson,
           London.

Powell, Dilys
    1973   *An Affair of the Heart*. Efstathiadis Group, Athens (originally
           published 1957).
    2001   *The Villa Ariadne*. Akadine Press (originally published 1973).

Preziosi, Donald
    2002   Archaeology as Museology: Re-thinking the Minoan Past. In
           Labyrinth Revisited, Rethinking 'Minoan' Archaeology, pp. 30–39.
           Edited by Yannis Hamilakis. Oxbow Books, Oxford.

Price, N.P.S.
    1994   Conservation and Information in the Display of Prehistoric Sites.
           In *The Politics of the Past*, pp. 284–290. Edited by Peter Gathercole
           and David Lowenthal. Routledge, London.

Rackham, Oliver and Jennifer Moody
    1996   *The Making of the Cretan Landscape*. Manchester University Press,
           Manchester.

Rehak, Paul and John G. Younger
    2001   Addendum: 1998: 1999. In *Aegean Prehistory: A Review,* pp. 466–473.
            Edited by Tracey Cullen. *American Journal of Archaeology Supplement*
            1 Archaeological Institute of America, Boston.

Renault, Mary
    1958   *The King Must Die.* Pantheon Books, New York.

Renfrew, Colin
    1972   *The Emergence of Civilization: The Cyclades and the Aegean in the*
            Third Millennium. Methuen, London.
    2003   Retrospect and Prospect: Mediterranean Archaeology in a New
            Millennium. In *Theory and Practice in Mediterranean Archaeology:*
            Old World and New World Perspectives, pp. 311–318. Edited by John
            K. Papadopoulos and Richard M. Leventhal. Cotsen Advanced
            Seminars 1. The Cotsen Institute of Archaeology.

Richards, G.
    1994   Developments in European Cultural Tourism. In *Tourism: The State*
            of the Art, pp. 366–376. Edited by A.V. Seaton. John Wiley, Chichester.

Rojek, Chris and John Urry
    1997   Transformations of Travel and Theory. In *Touring Cultures:*
            Transformations of Travel and Theory, pp. 1–19. Edited by Chris
            Rojek and John Urry. Routledge, London.

Rossiter, Stuart
    1980   *The Blue Guides. Greece.* Ernest Benn, London.

Rough Guide to Greece
    1998   Rough Guide Publications Ltd, London.

Russell, Ian
    2006   Images of the Past: Archaeologies, Modernities, Crises and Poetics.
            In *Images, Representations and Heritage,* pp. 1–38. Edited by Ian
            Russell. Springer, New York.

Ryan, Jake and Charles Sackrey
    1996   *Strangers in Paradise: Academics from the Working Class.* University
            Press of America, Lanham, MD.

Said, Edward
    1978   *Orientalism.* Pantheon Books, New York.

Sahlins, Marshall
    1968   *Tribesman.* Prentice Hall, Englewood Cliffs, New Jersey.

Sakellarakis, Yannis and Efi Sakellarakis
    1992a Archanes-Phourni. In *The Aerial Atlas of Ancient Crete,* pp. 54–58.
            Edited by J. Wilson Myers, E.E. Myers, and G. Cadogan. Thames
            and Hudson, London.
    1992b Archanes-Tourkoyeitonia. In *The Aerial Atlas of Ancient Crete,* pp.
            59–62. Edited by J. Wilson Myers, E.E. Myers, and G. Cadogan.
            Thames and Hudson, London.

Service, Elman
 1962 *Primitive Social Organization: An Evolutionary Perspective.* Random House, New York.
Shanks, Michael
 1992 *Experiencing Archaeology.* Routledge, London.
 2001 Culture/Archaeology. The Dispersion of a Discipline and Its Objects. In *Archaeological Theory Today*, pp. 285–305. Edited by Ian Hodder. Polity Press, Cambridge.
 2004 Three Rooms: "Archaeology and Performance." *Journal of Social Archaeology* 4:147–180.
Shanks, Michael and Christopher Tilley
 1987 *Re-Constructing Archaeology.* Cambridge University Press, Cambridge.
Shaw, Joseph W.
 1992 Kommos. In *The Aerial Atlas of Ancient Crete*, pp. 149–153. Edited by J. Wilson Myers, E.E. Myers and G. Cadogan. Thames and Hudson, London.
 2006 *Kommos: A Minoan Harbor Town and Greek Sanctuary in Southern Crete.* Mystis, Iraklio, Crete.
Sherratt, Andrew
 2006 Crete, Greece, and the Orient in the Thought of Gordon Childe (with an Appendix on Toynbee and Spengler: The Afterlife of the Minoans in European Intellectual History). In "Archaeology and European Modernity: Producing and Consuming the 'Minoans'," pp. 107–126. Edited by Yannis Hamilakis and Nicoletta Momigliano *Creta Antica* 7. Bottega d'Erasmo, Aldo Ausilio, Padua.
Sherratt, Andrew and Susan Sherratt
 1991 From Luxuries to Commodities: The Nature of Mediterranean Bronze Age Trading Systems. In *Bronze Age Trade in the Mediterranean. Paper Presented at the Conference Held in Rewley House, Oxford, in December 1989*, pp. 351–386. Edited by N.H. Gale. Paul Åströms Förlag. Shoep, Ilse.
 2002 The State of the Minoan Palaces or the Minoan Palace-State? In *Monuments of Minos: Rethinking the Minoan Palaces*, pp. 15–33. Edited by Jan Driessen, Ilse Schoep, and Robert Laffineur. *Aegaeum* 23. Annales d'Archéologie Égéenne de l'Université de Liège et UT-PASAP.
Silberman, Neil Asher
 1989 *Between Past and Present: Archaeology, Ideology, and Nationalism in the Modern Middle East.* Anchor Books, New York.
 1995 Promised Lands and Chosen Peoples: The Politics and Poetics of Archaeological Narrative. In *Nationalism, Politics, and the Practice of Archaeology*, pp. 249–262. Edited by Philip L. Kohl and Clare Fawcett. Cambridge University Press, Cambridge.
Silverman, Helaine
 2002 Touring Ancient Times: The Present and Presented Past in Contemporary Peru. *American Anthropologist* 104:881–902.

2006   *Archaeological Site Museums in Latin America*. University Press of Florida, Gainesville (editor).

Simandiraki, Anna
2006   The Minoan Experience of Schoolchildren in Crete. In "Archaeology and European Modernity: Producing and Consuming the 'Minoans'," pp. 259–274. Edited by Yannis Hamilakis and Nicoletta Momogliano. *Creta Antica* 7. Bottega d'Erasmo, Aldo Ausilio, Padua.

Simmel, G.
1978   *The Philosophy of Money*. Routledge, London.

Smith, Anthony
1971   *Theories of Nationalism*. Harper and Row, New York.

Smith, Valene L.
1989   Introduction. In *Hosts and Guests: The Anthropology of Tourism*, pp. 1–17. Edited by Valene L. Smith. University of Pennsylvania Press, Philadelphia.

Soles, Jeffrey S.
2002   A Central Court at Gournia? In *Monuments of Minos: Rethinking the Minoan Palaces*, pp. 123–132. Edited by Jan Driessen, Ilse Schoep, and Robert Laffineur. *Aegaeum* 23. Annales d'Archéologie Égéenne de l'Université de Liège et UT-PASAP.

Solomon, Esther
2006   Knossos: Social Uses of a Monumental Landscape. In "Archaeology and European Modernity: Producing and Consuming the 'Minoans'," pp. 163–182. Edited by Yannis Hamilakis and Nicoletta Momogliano. *Creta Antica* 7. Bottega d'Erasmo, Aldo Ausilio, Padua.

Stanley-Price, Nicholas
2003   Site Preservation and Archaeology in the Mediterranean Region. In *Theory and Practice in Mediterranean Archaeology: Old World and New World Perspectives*, pp. 269–283. Edited by John K. Papadopoulos and Richard M. Leventhal. Cotsen Advanced Seminars 1. The Cotsen Institute of Archaeology.

Stone, P.G. and B. Molyneux (editors)
1994   *The Presented Past: Heritage, Museums and Education*. Unwin and Hyman, London.

Stritch, Deirdre
2006   Archaeological Tourism as a Signpost to National Identity. In *Images, Representations and Heritage*, pp. 43–60. Edited by Ian Russell. Springer, New York.

Thomas, Nicholas
1994   *Colonialism's Culture*. Princeton University Press, Princeton, NJ.

Tilley, Christopher
1993   *Interpretative Archaeology*. Berg, Oxford.
2004   Round Barrows and Dykes as Landscape Metaphors. *Cambridge Archaeological Journal* 14:185–203.

Trigger, Bruce
    1984   Alternative Archaeologies: Nationalist, Colonialist, Imperialist. *Man* 19:355–370.
    1989   *A History of Archaeological Thought*. Cambridge University Press, Cambridge.
    1995   Romanticism, Nationalism, and Archaeology. In *Nationalism, Politics, and the Practice of Archaeology*, pp. 263–279. Edited by Philip L. Kohl and Clare Fawcett. Cambridge University Press, Cambridge.

Tsipopoulou, Metaxia
    2002   Petras, Siteia: The Palace, the Town, the Hinterland and the Protopalatial Background. In *Monuments of Minos: Rethinking the Minoan Palaces*, pp. 133–144. Edited by Jan Driessen, Ilse Schoep, and Robert Laffineur. *Aegaeum* 23. Annales d'Archéologie Égéenne de l'Université de Liège et UT-PASAP.
    2003   The Minoan Palace at Petras, Siteia. *Athena Review* 3. On-line version www.athenapub.com.

Tylor, E.B.
    1865   *Researches into the Early History of Mankind and the Development of Civilization*. John Murray, London.

Tzedakis, Yannis
    1992   Armeni. In *The Aerial Atlas of Ancient Crete*, pp. 63–65. Edited by J. Wilson Myers, E.E. Myers, and G. Cadogan. Thames and Hudson, London.

Unsworth, Barry
    2004   *Crete*. National Geographic Society, Washington, DC.

Urry, John
    1990   *The Tourist Gaze: Leisure and Travel in Contemporary Societies*. Sage Publications, London.

Van Effenterre, Henri and Micheline van Effenterre
    1997   Toward a Study of Neopalatial "Villas": Modern Words for Minoan Things. In *The Function of the "Minoan Villa,"* pp. 9–13. Edited by Robin Hägg. Paul Åströms Förlag.

Vasilakis, Antonis
    1992   Tylissos. In *The Aerial Atlas of Ancient Crete*, pp. 272–275. Edited by J. Wilson Myers, E.E. Myers and G. Cadogan. Thames and Hudson, London.

Voyatzis, Mary E.
    1999   From Athena to Zeus: An A–Z Guide to the Origins of Greek Goddesses. The Sacred World of the Minoans. In *Ancient Goddesses*, pp. 133–147. Edited by Lucy Goodison and Christine Morris. The University of Wisconsin Press, Madison.

Wallace, Saro
    2005   Bridges in the Mountains: Issues of Structure, Multi-Vocality, Responsibility and Gain in Filling a Management Gap in Rural Greece. *Journal of Mediterranean Archaeology* 18:55–85.

Ware, Cheryl L.
2003 The Value of Travel Literature in a Global Society. *International Journal of the Humanities* 1:1753–1762.

Warren, Peter
2000 Early Travellers from Britain and Ireland. In *Cretan Quests: British Explorers, Excavators and Historians*, pp. 1–8. Edited by Davina Huxley. British School at Athens, London.
2002 Political Structure in Neopalatial Crete. In *Monuments of Minos: Rethinking the Minoan Palaces*, pp. 201–205. Edited by Jan Driessen, Ilse Schoep, and Robert Laffineur. *Aegaeum* 23. Annales d'Archéologie Égéenne de l'Université de Liège et UT-PASAP.

Watrous, L. Vance
2001 Crete from Earliest Prehistory through the Protopalatial Period. Addendum 1994–1999. In *Aegean Prehistory: A Review*. Edited by Tracey Cullen, pp. 157–223. *American Journal of Archaeology Supplement 1*. Archaeological Institute of America, Boston.

White, Leslie A.
1959 *The Evolution of Culture*. McGraw-Hill, New York.

Wickens, E.
1994 Consumption of the Authentic: The Hedonistic Tourist in Greece. In *Tourism: The State of the Art*, pp. 818–825. Edited by A. V. Seaton, Wiley and Sons, New York.

Wilkie, Laurie A. and Kevin M. Bartoy
2000 A Critical Archaeology Revisited. *Current Anthropology* 41:747–777.

Williams, Wendy and Elly Maria Papamichael.
1995 Tourism and Tradition: Local Control versus Outside Interests in Greece. In *International Tourism: Identity and Change*, pp. 127–142. Edited by Marie-Françoise Lanfant, John B. Allcock, and Edward M. Bruner. Sage Publications, Thousand Oaks, CA.

Wolf, Eric
1982 *Europe and the People Without History*. University of California Press, Berkeley.

Wylie, Alison
1992 The Interplay of Evidential Constraints and Political Interests: Recent Archaeological Research on Gender. *American Antiquity* 57:15–35.
2002 *Thinking from Things: Essays in the Philosophy of Archaeology* University of California Press, Berkeley.

Zois, Antonis
1990 *Archaeology in Greece: Realities and Prospects*. Polytypo, Athens.

A P P E N D I X

Site Gazetteer

The descriptions that follow are based on a number of published sources. The comments accompanying each site description are taken from my field notes during visits to the sites made mostly in March and April of 2002.

Agia Triada

Archaeology

Type: Settlement with associated cemetery

Date: EM I–LM IIIC

Description: A settlement complex with a villa that dates to the Middle Minoan period. During the Late Minoan period it eclipsed the nearby palace of Phaistos. Northeast of the site are two tholos tombs (La Rosa 1992a).

Comments

The site is well signposted although the road to the site from the main road was not drivable, so you have to take the longer route around Phaistos. The site brochure covers the chronological periods and the site's changing architecture. A final paragraph covers the spectacular finds. There are no information plaques on the site and no path to take you around it and through it. There is nothing to stop you walking on the walls; in fact, it is almost impossible not to if you want to cover the whole site. A minor disappointment was the tombs to the north of the site, which had been described in every guidebook, were locked up, and the attendant did not have the key.

Amnisos

Archaeology

Type: Villa

Date: LM

Description: A two-story building that probably served as the home of an official of the nearby harbor (Davaras 1976).

Comments

The site is not well looked after. Both of the complexes at the base of the hill are fenced off. The hilltop complex is overgrown and unmarked. The whole site is surrounded by detritus and garbage and an abandoned caravan.

Armeni

Archaeology

Type: Cemetery

Date: LM IIIA–IIIB

Description: A cemetery consisting of over two hundred chamber tombs with tholoi cut into the bedrock. A Minoan road runs through the cemetery (Tzedakis 1992).

Comments

The site was well signposted off the main Rethymno/Spili highway. It is open from 8 am to 3 pm. On-site "curator." The excavated graves are open. There is a walkway through the site but there is no problem in walking wherever you want. There is no "signage" on site and no site brochure was available.

Chamaizi

Archaeology

Type: Country dwelling or villa

Date: EM–MM IA

Description: A circular building on the crest of a hill commanding a wide view of the surrounding countryside. Its shape was probably dictated by the confines of the hill itself (Davaras 1992).

Comments

We visited this site just because we were driving along the main highway and saw the sign. A very poor cart track took us to the site. It has a spectacular view, but there is absolutely no on-site information at all.

Chania

Archaeology

Type: Settlement with possible palace

Date: EM–LM IIIC

Description: A site complex with a major palace, although a central court has not yet been found (*Athena Review* 2003d).

Comments

The Minoan site actually covers a large area of the hill but because of the intense development of the hill we were able to view only one section of the town. The site is not well signposted, and there is only one sign at the site itself. There is, however, an information plaque that shows the layout of the site, its main chronological periods, and the history of the excavations.

Gournia

Archaeology

Type: Town

Date: EM II–LM IIIB

Description: A coastal town boasting a regional palace (though some dispute this status) that dates to the LMI period. The remains comprise well laid-out streets and the basements of houses (Cadogan 1992b).

Comments

This site offers the visitor a sense of how regular people lived and is thus a necessary antidote to the sumptuous palaces on the main tourist trail. It could be used very actively to show the "other side" of Minoan life. The site is well signposted off the national road and access is by a track that wends through an olive grove. The site was manned by a single curator who seemed unwilling (or unable?) to offer any information on the site. The site had very poor signs that really did not help the visitor understand its history and importance.

Kato Zakro

Archaeology

Type: Palace and associated town

Date: EM III–LM I

Description: The site is found on the east coast of the island. The palace sits at the eastern end of a small valley with the Minoan town on hills to either side (Platon 1992).

Comments

An important site, but it lacks a good system of signage. The site has a few on-site signs although the brochure map is adequate. There is no museum or other facilities.

Knossos

Archaeology

Type: Palace

Date: EM I–LM IIIC

Description: One of the four great palaces of Minoan Crete. The palace itself is surrounded by a large complex of associated buildings and features, most of which are not open to the public (Cadogan 1992c). Macdonald (2003) suggests three building phases with the New Palace Period, each one necessitated by earthquake damage. The original New Palace was built in MMIIIB (1700–1600 B.C.) after the destruction of the Old Palace. The Frescoed Palace was built at the beginning of the LMIA (1600 B.C.), and the Ruined Palace, which contains no signs of occupation, was in use as a ceremonial center during LMIB up until 1450 B.C., when rebuilding was interrupted by yet another earthquake and it was converted into a Mycenaean palace.

Comments

This site is one of the most popular tourist attractions on the island. It is the most developed of the sites in terms of tourist facilities. The reconstruction by Evans—regardless of its specific accuracy—gives the visitor a good taste of what these palaces might have looked like. Until 2004 the on-site signs were not particularly informative. However, it now boasts much more informative signs.

Kommos

Archaeology

Type: Settlement

Date: MM–LM III

Description: This settlement was no doubt associated with the port of Kommos, which was probably the chief harbor for Phaistos (Shaw 1992).

Comments

The site was fenced off with no access possible. There were no informational signs.

Mallia

Archaeology

Type: Palace with associated town and cemetery

Date: EM II LM IIIB/C

Description: One of the four great palaces of Minoan Crete. It is surrounded by a town. The Chrysolakkos cemetery lies to the north of the complex (Pelon et al. 1992).

Comments

There is minimal on-site interpretation. However, there is an excellent gallery, showing photographs of the excavations and giving a very good summary of the site. Whether most visitors go there is, however, another matter. Important parts of the site were closed.

Nirou Khani

Archaeology

Type: Villa

Date: LM IA

Description: This villa sits close to Amnisos and is also associated with a small harbor. The courtyard is surrounded by residential and storage rooms. Four huge bronze double axes were among the objects found there (Davaras 1976).

Comments

The site is on the old National Road and so is clearly visible. It was fenced off and unfortunately the keyholder was nowhere to be found. Part of the site is roofed over. There is a carving on a rock of the site's plan at the entrance to the site.

Palaikastro (Roussolakos)

Archaeology

Type: Town

Date: EM IB–LM IIIB

Description: A well laid-out town indicative of a prosperous economy, probably based on maritime trade, olive production, and sheep rearing (MacGillivray and Sackett 1992).

Comments

This site is very well signposted from the main highway. The site has excellent on-site signs, which provide good site maps and clear information on the dates of the individual components and the site's construction history.

Phaistos

Archaeology

Type: Palace

Date: EM II–LM IB

Description: One of the four great palaces of Minoan Crete. Perhaps only Knossos was more important. The site overlooks the fertile Plain of Mesara (La Rosa 1992b).

Comments

There were no informational signs on the site or guides available for hire. The small brochure shows the periods of occupation from Neolithic to Hellenic. The site has a gift shop and museum shop. A good range of books on Phaistos, Crete, and Greece is available. The site has been stabilized but not restored like Knossos, which gives the visitor an unimpeded view of the countryside.

Phourni (Archanes)

Archaeology

Type: Cemetery

Date: EM II–Sub Minoan

Description: A very important prehistoric cemetery—perhaps the most important in the Aegean according to the Sakellarakises—containing twenty-four funerary structures of different types, including shaft graves and tholoi, plus one secular building (Sakellarakis and Sakellarakis 1992a).

Comments

This site is not well advertised and the signs from the highway are not clear; nor do they indicate how far away it is from the turnoff. It was difficult to find all the different structures because there is no site map.

The curator in the booth was very reticent to speak to any of the visitors at first but I persevered and finally got some good information from him about the site. He spoke with near reverence for the site's excavator, Yannis Sakellarakis.

Sklavokambos

Archaeology

Type: Villa

Date: LM I

Description: A two-story villa comprising a small central courtyard, swelling rooms, and storage rooms (Davaras 1976).

Comments

The site is easy to find as it is on the main highway, but the signpost is small. The site is fenced and closed and no on-site information is available. It is even more difficult to visit because the site has no place in which to park and there is virtually no hard shoulder to the road.

Tourkogeitonia

Archaeology

Type: Settlement and palatial building

Date: MM IIB–LM I.

Description: A well-built palatial structure of the same quality as the four major palaces, although it has a different plan (Sakellarakis and Sakellarakis 1992b).

Comments

Excavations are ongoing. It was very difficult to find the site as there are no signs. The site was closed but could be viewed through the wire fence (3/4/02).

Tylissos

Archaeology

Type: Town

Date: EM II–LM III

Description: Only a small portion of the town has been excavated. Two large houses have been uncovered as well as a smaller house possibly used for storage (Vasilakis 1992).

Comments

The site was not well marked and appeared rather unkempt. Free parking was to be had in the courtyard of an adjacent house. A matriarch tried (successfully) to sell us her homemade lace ware.

Vathypetro

Archaeology

Type: Villa and rural outbuildings

Date: LM I

Description: This villa shows some of the features to be found in a country house, such as a wine/oil press and the large number of storage pithoi (Cadogan 1992d).

Comments

The site has been closed more than open on the times I have visited it.

MUSEUMS

Agios Nikolaos

A well laid-out modern museum complex. The lighting is excellent. Very difficult to get to if arriving by car because of the problems of parking in the town during the summer months.

Archanes

A simple affair. Good layout. Lots of informational plaques that are well presented.

Chania

The museum is in what was once a beautiful Catholic church. It is one of the most beautiful settings for a museum. As a Rethymno, there is a very good map of the sites in Chania province and then the visitor is left to wander through the different periods. The whole museum is in essentially one large room and so you are not "guided." However, I was impressed by the descriptive notes with each cabinet of finds. They were brief but took you beyond the "bare facts." What stood out was the regular reference to male vs. female in the tomb offerings.

Iraklio

The *treasure palace* of Minoan Crete. The different galleries are laid out on a chronological basis. There seems to have been little rotation of materials. The accompanying plaques are not particularly informative, so the purchase of a guide book is a necessity. In the summer the crowds of tourists make it almost unbearable.

Rethymno

This will be the first of several visits, I am sure, but I did want to get a first impression. I was very impressed. The museum occupies one large room. The first display is a map of the different types of sites in the Rethymno area. Then you proceed to wall cases that take you through the various periods—from Neolithic to Roman. Most of the artifacts are pottery, but there are bone tools on display, and there are some some excellent larnaces.

Siteia

These small museums are the gems of the Archaeological Service. The lighting at Siteia is natural, and there is an excellent range of artifacts from the Linear A tablets of Kato Zakro to everyday utensils. The entry to the museum also has a very good display on the chronology of the area and on the range of sites found in the surrounding district.

INDEX

ABOUT THE AUTHOR

Philip Duke is professor of anthropology at Fort Lewis College, Durango, Colorado, where he has taught since 1980. He is a Fellow of the Society of Antiquaries. Until recently, his professional work has been conducted on the archaeology of western North America, about which he has written numerous articles and monographs. He is the author of, amongst other books, *Points in Time: Structure and Event in a Late Northern Plains Hunting Society.* He is the co-editor of *Beyond Subsistence: Plains Archaeology and the Postprocessual Critique* (with Michael Wilson), and the forthcoming *Archaeology and Capitalism: From Ethics to Politics* (with Yannis Hamilakis). His research specialties include public archaeology, and repatriation and heritage issues, and it is these that have taken him back to his first love, Greek archaeology. He also works with the Ludlow Collective at the archaeological site of the 1914 Ludlow massacre near Trinidad, Colorado.